M000306693

EMERGENCY MANAGEMENT

for Records and Information Programs

2nd Edition

Virginia A. Jones, CRM, FAI and Darlene Barber, CRM

ARMA

INTERNATIONAL®

ARMA International
Overland Park, Kansas

Consulting Editor: Mary L. Ginn, Ph.D.
Composition: Cole Design & Production
Cover Art: Brett Dietrich

ARMA International
11880 College Blvd., Ste. 450
Overland Park, KS 66210
913.341.3808

©2011 by ARMA International. All rights reserved.
Printed in the United States of America.

The text of this publication, or any part thereof, may not be reproduced
without the written permission of ARMA International.

ISBN: 978-1-936654-01-7
Catalog No. A4914

Contents

Acknowledgments

The authors wish to acknowledge the help of their records and information management colleagues in obtaining resources on the subject matter of this book. They also acknowledge the significant contribution of Kris E. Keyes to the first edition of this book and the continued importance of the emergency management information he authored.

Introduction

Most leaders of organizations are aware that an emergency that may disrupt operations and destroy critical records and information can occur. Global incidents over the past few years have shown that many organizations will not recover from a major disaster. In a 2002 study, the research firm, Gartner, reported that 40 percent of small- and mid-sized companies that experience a sudden misfortune go out of business within five years.[1]

According to Gartner Research, a 20-year survey of Fortune 500 crisis readiness by the University of Southern California's Center for Crisis Management demonstrated two troubling conclusions: (1) the incidence of intentional damage to corporate assets has risen markedly during the past 10 years, and (2) between 75 and 95 percent of Fortune 500 companies are not prepared to manage a new type of crisis.[2]

Emergency Management for Records and Information Programs was written to assist records managers, information technology managers, risk managers, compliance managers, and all who are responsible for the protection of their organization's information resources. The primary objective is to help prevent records and information emergencies from becoming disasters that result in great destruction or irreplaceable loss. Therefore, the text is organized as a guide through the essential phases of emergency management—mitigation (prevention), preparedness, response, and recovery—with an emphasis on mitigation and preparation. This book can be used as a companion to ANSI/ARMA 5-2010, *Vital Records: Identifying, Managing, and Recovering Business-Critical Records.*

While the term *emergency management* best describes government practices and procedures for responding to community-wide disasters and disruptive events, the same concepts are used to form the basis of business continuity planning. This edition looks at protection and loss recovery management for records and information from a risk management perspective and includes legal compliance, electronic security, and data privacy risk, as well as acts of nature and technological or social emergency events. Material presented in each section is not comprehensive. More information can be found in texts that are geared specifically toward each topic covered in the book.

- Section I sets the foundation by discussing the basic concepts of emergency management and of business continuity planning (BCP), the role of records and information management in both emergency business continuity management and business process analysis, and insight on selling the need for business continuity and emergency management to organizational management.

- Section II addresses the mitigation phase of records and information emergency management and business continuity—risk management, vital records, and loss prevention planning.

DISASTER SNAPSHOT

During the Loma Preita, California, earthquake in October 1989, business interruption caused $5 billion in damage. Many small businesses still found recovering difficult. Even those that did not suffer extreme physical damage were closed while officials conducted safety inspections. Many business owners were not permitted to retrieve paperwork, equipment, or anything for several days. A San Francisco newspaper estimated that up to 25 percent of the smaller companies in stricken areas would be forced to close.

Source: Janette Ballman, "Then and Now! Small Businesses Are Finding It Difficult to Recover." *Disaster Recovery Journal* 7, no. 2 (April/May/June 1994): 34.

- Section III addresses the preparedness phase and discusses business continuity planning and preparing a records and information emergency management plan.

- Section IV addresses the response phase of activating the emergency management and business continuity plan.

- Section V addresses the recovery phase and resumption of operations and subsequent actions.

Organizational leaders sometimes approach emergency management and business continuity in a piecemeal manner. Some organizations may have a policy on telecommuting during a pandemic, or may adopt board resolutions on cooperation with local authorities during emergencies. Manufacturers may maintain lists of alternative suppliers or shipping sources, and information systems departments may faithfully perform back-up procedures. Many organizations, though, do not have a *comprehensive* plan for managing disruptive events and preventing loss that includes all four phases of emergency management or the continuity of business operations following a disruptive event.

A 2010 national Business Continuity Study by AT&T included 530 IT executives in five U.S. metropolitan/regional areas that responded to an online survey. Respondents from companies in Detroit (Midwest); San Francisco/San Ramon (West); Philadelphia/Pittsburgh (East); Missouri (Central); and Louisiana/Mississippi/Alabama/Florida (Gulf Coast) with total revenues of at least $10 million (except for state/local governments) had primary responsibility for business continuity planning, and they represented fourteen major industry areas and local/state governments.

The study explored the importance of business continuity plans with any additional requirements that companies had regarding the plans, especially as it related to emerging technologies. Most IT executives expressed concerns about the increased usage of social networking capabilities and mobile networks/devices and their potential impact on security threats.

The key findings of the study include:

- Business continuity planning was seen as a priority by three out of four (76%) IT executives; half (50%) indicated that it had been a priority for their businesses; and one-fourth (26%) indicated that it had become a priority in recent years because of natural disasters, security, and terrorist threats.

- Eight out of ten (83%) executives indicated that their companies had a business continuity plan; one out of two (12%) indicated that their companies did not have a plan; and 5% did not know whether a plan was in place.

- A majority (54%) had fully tested their business continuity plans in the past year; almost one-fifth (17%) last fully tested their plans more than a year ago; and 6% indicated that their plans had never been fully tested.

- Nationally, six out of ten (62%) companies implemented specific protective actions when the federal or state government issued an alert for an impending disaster.

- Three out of four (72%) executives indicated that their company had prioritized and set target recovery times for each key business process.

- Nationally, three out of ten (29%) companies had ever invoked their business continuity plan.

- Nationally, power outages at facilities or extreme weather were the primary reasons for invoking business continuity plans; U.S. Gulf Coast companies were significantly more likely to invoke their plans for extreme weather.[3]

Without critical records and information, an organization has difficulty serving its customers, securing new customers, manufacturing products, borrowing money, collecting debts from creditors, justifying tax liability to the government, enforcing contracts, defending itself against liability lawsuits, keeping the goodwill and

DISASTER SNAPSHOT

A secretary was eager to use a friend's software program and installed it as a surprise for her supervisor. While installing the unauthorized copy of software, she inadvertently overwrote data on the computer's hard drive and thus destroyed all the company's data.

Source: Carleen Bridgeman, "Foolproof Solutions for the Foolhardy," *Disaster Recovery Journal* 7, no. 2 (April/May/June 1994): 77.

loyalty of its customer base, proving compliance with government regulations, or even substantiating losses it has sustained on insurance claims.[4]

Records and information business continuity and emergency management plans should represent the organization's leaders' efforts to *protect* records and information from loss, their ability to *prevent* the loss of records and information, their ability to *respond* to a disruptive event in any of the organization's offices or facilities, and their ability to *recover* as quickly as possible following a disruptive event.

> **DISASTER SNAPSHOT**
>
> A dentist's office in Albuquerque, New Mexico, housed its files in an alcove file room off the main reception area. A large fish tank was located between the alcove and the patient waiting area. During a three-day weekend, an electrical short in the fish tank caused a fire that destroyed patient records.
>
> *Source:* Robert Gianninni, DDS, Albuquerque, New Mexico, interview with Virginia Jones, 12 February 1991.

Small businesses and organizations are especially susceptible to major loss from disasters. They can rarely support the costs associated with establishing complex routine back-up procedures, maintaining alternative operating sites, or routinely testing emergency management and business continuity plans. To remain competitive with large organizations with greater resources, small organizations must rebuild quickly with fewer resources and a smaller work force. The strategies described in this book can be applied to any organization, regardless of size.

Organizations of all sizes and industry types can find helpful information in the sidebars in each chapter called *Quick Tips*. Brief scenarios of actual records and information disasters are presented throughout the text in a special feature called *Disaster Snapshot*. Additional scenarios of actual disaster response and the results of subsequent review of both positive and difficult consequences, called *Lesson Learned*, are also found in each chapter. Each chapter contains a checklist of important steps to follow during each phase of the preparation of an emergency management and business continuity plan.

A Glossary of important terms is included in Appendix A. Additional information and other related publications can be found in the Selected Bibliography in Appendix B. A large amount of detailed procedures for recovering or salvaging damaged records and information cannot be a part of this publication due to space limitations. References to publications on these topics are also found in Appendix B. Sample forms are provided in Appendix C.

For the sake of simplicity, the authors have used literary license with several terms. *Emergency management plan* is used in place of the longer term *emergency management prevention and recovery plan*. *Organization* is used to mean any government agency or department and any private business or company. *Records* and *records and information* are used interchangeably to mean records and information in any form.

References are made to United States regulatory and relief agencies throughout this publication. Readers outside the United States may benefit by researching the requirements of similar agencies within their governments.

NOTES

1. Cathleen Ferraro, "Avoiding Data Disaster: Many small businesses fail to protect their core documents from the threat of calamity." *The Sacramento Bee* (4 June 2003): 1.

2. Kristen Noakes-Fry and Trude Diamond, "Business Continuity and Disaster Recovery Planning and Management: Technology Overview," Gartner, Inc. (11 July 2003): 2.

3. 2010 AT&T Business Continuity Study, U.S. National Results (2010). 7 May 2011 <http://www.att.com/gen/press-room?pid=17839#statelinks> and <http://www.att.com/common/about_us/files/business_continuity/BusinessContinuity_2010_Summary.pdf>.

4. Mary F. Robek, Gerald F. Brown, and David O. Stephens, *Information and Records Management: Document Based Information Systems,* 4th ed. (New York: Glencoe/McGraw-Hill, Inc., 1995), 68.

SECTION I:
BASIC CONCEPTS

Emergency management and business continuity planning are planned approaches to the prevention of disasters, preparedness and response to disruptive events, and recovery following a disruptive event. Understanding emergency management and business continuity concepts, and the impact of certain records and information management concepts on emergency management and business continuity, is necessary for developing effective records and information emergency management and business continuity plans.

Emergency Management Concepts

"Anything that can cause a disruption in the normal operation of your business can be a disaster."[1]

The first step in the study of emergency management and the development of a comprehensive emergency management plan for records and information is to understand the concepts of emergencies and disasters. Records and information are best protected by strong, cost-efficient emergency management and business continuity plans.

An **emergency** is a sudden, urgent, usually unexpected occurrence or occasion requiring immediate action. Examples of an emergency include: a broken water pipe, a bomb threat, a severe storm, a data security breach, or other events that require actions but do not necessarily require significant efforts to control. This event does not usually result in major loss for an organization.

A **disaster,** on the other hand, is an emergency event that progresses from the realm of standard operating procedures to conditions requiring resources often beyond the organization's means. Disasters result in significant financial and operational damage and loss. Examples of disasters include: a fire that destroys a facility, a flood that causes major facility and product loss, and a tornado that causes major damage to one or more facilities and/or product loss. A disaster can be a small but localized event, such as a major fire to a business, or a widespread event, such as a natural disaster, that causes significant damage to a community.

Jeffrey Bumgarner, in *Emergency Management,* discusses three categories of disasters (or hazards): natural, technological, and social.[2] He describes **natural disasters,** or acts of nature, as geological (earthquakes), meteorological (hurricanes, tornadoes), hydrological (floods) and biological (disease pandemics).[3] Each geographic region is subject to particular natural disasters. Although such disasters cannot be averted, more accurate forecasting and sophisticated warning systems have reduced the unexpectedness of some natural disasters. The primary loss prevention measures for natural disasters are good planning and preparation.

Technological disasters are events usually caused by human error or as secondary occurrences to natural disasters. Technical disasters can include the release of hazardous materials, airplane crashes, structural failures, a security breach of data, a viral attack on the computer network, and dam failures. Collapsed buildings from an earthquake or major fire can cause the release of hazardous materials or radiation emissions. Building and equipment failure or malfunction may cause fire and flooding. Electrical malfunctions, such as defective wiring, overheated motors, and faulty switch boxes, and controllers, are the primary cause of business fires.[4]

Unlike natural disasters, technical disasters can be avoided. The mitigation part of a business continuity or emergency management plan should address potential problem areas and describe technological security, inspection, and maintenance practices that significantly reduce the danger of technological hazards.

Human error or carelessness is often the cause of fire, theft, misinformation, and information loss. It can be prevented through employee training, adequate supervision, implementing security measures, and a constant sensitivity to potential hazards. Theft is a common problem that plagues every aspect of organizational life including information. Industrial espionage can cause significant financial loss from stolen designs and lost patent opportunities.

Social disasters are deliberate destructive activities causing illness, injury, and death. The scope of a social disaster can vary from a localized event to one with widespread destruction. Social disasters are unpredictable and can occur anywhere at any time. Acts of deliberate destructiveness include theft, espionage, vandalism, riots, terrorism, and war. Terrorism and vandalism are occurring more frequently throughout the world. Protection of records and information from acts of deliberate destructiveness is addressed primarily through application of appropriate safety and security measures. Losses from these types of disasters can be greatly reduced through adequate planning measures and implementing a loss prevention plan.

The scope of emergencies or disasters can be **community-wide events** with immediate disruption of communications and emergency services, power outages, and widespread destruction. In a community-wide disaster, employees' homes and families are often endangered and take priority over organization responsibilities. Community-wide disasters create conditions that hinder the access to and restoration of back-up information. They also pose difficulties in getting to facilities and work sites to begin records and information recovery processes.

Localized events may also include loss of life, power outages, and massive destruction; but communications and emergency services may not be affected. Localized events allow quick application of back-up procedures, although they may still hinder the start of records salvage operations. A localized event may be a tornado, a localized flood, or a bombing incident.

Organizational events strike only a single building, floor, office, or organization, and because of the narrow scope of these events, greater use of community and organization resources is possible. Applying response and recovery procedures and accessing damaged areas to begin recovery can usually be accomplished quickly. Examples of organizational events are fires, burst water pipes, breach of computer network security, or power failures.

Emergency Management

Emergency management is a planned approach for the prevention of disasters, preparedness and response to emergencies, and recovery following an emergency or disaster. Most important to any effort to safeguard records and information is to include records and information in asset protection plans. A plan for records and information should be considered a part of the organization's emergency management and business continuity plans. Organization personnel must assess risk, secure facilities, deploy resources, and conduct other activities to be successful at mitigating loss.

Emergency management professionals define four distinct programs or phases of a comprehensive emergency management plan. These four phases are mitigation (prevention), preparedness, response, and recovery.[5] While some people believe that prevention and recovery alone make up a sound plan, others believe that preparedness and recovery are the only necessary elements of a sound plan. The most effective plans include the four-phase approach.

Mitigation

The first phase of a comprehensive emergency management plan is to take steps to prevent records and information disasters from occurring. *Risk management, risk aversion,* and *loss prevention* are other terms used for the mitigation phase of emergency management. **Mitigation** is the activities or measures taken to eliminate or reduce the probability of loss should a disruptive event occur. If events do occur, having mitigated known risks will reduce the chance of emergencies turning into records and information disasters.

Mitigation activities include identifying organizational elements that are at risk, the type and levels of risk, and the probability of risk (determining the likelihood that the risk will result in a disruptive event).[6] Risk management is discussed in greater length in Section II. Prevention initiatives can also include mitigating risk by performing activities such as installing a fire suppression system in a records storage center, finding and encapsulating water pipes placed above a technical library, and implementing data security procedures.

Preparedness

Being prepared is a prerequisite for response. Being prepared means having the organization's resources positioned before a disruptive event occurs. **Preparedness** includes the activities established to assist in responding to an event. A few examples of preparedness activities include developing and updating the emergency response plan, testing emergency systems, training personnel, stocking emergency supplies, lining up approved recovery vendors, and establishing hot or cold sites.[7]

Preparedness also means that personnel can recognize a disruptive event immediately and activate the emergency response plan. All the planning in the world cannot help an organization if its personnel cannot recognize a small problem before it develops into a disruptive event. Training, plan testing, and emergency simulation are vital to the success of the emergency response program. Section III presents more detail on exercising the plan and simulating emergencies.

Response

After someone recognizes an emergency or potential disruptive event, the emergency response plan is activated. **Response** includes the activities established to react immediately to an emergency event. Responding to an event means initiating resources necessary to protect or secure the organization from loss. Activities immediately before, during, or directly after events are *response activities*.[8]

Response activities include contacting the emergency response team, notifying appropriate authorities, securing facilities, issuing press releases, activating emergency response systems, and notifying records and information recovery resources. At this point, the emergency management plan leads into the recovery phase. Section IV covers the response phase in more detail.

Recovery

Recovery includes activities associated with restoring resources or operations following a disruptive event. It involves all activities necessary to restore the organization's systems and processes to normal operating status. Recovery phase activities can include dehumidifying records, restoring information onto computers, and returning vital records from offsite emergency storage. The organization can divide the recovery process into two phases, depending on the extent of the loss.[9]

Usually, the short-term recovery phase involves the restoration of vital systems and processes that can get the organization's mission, product, or service back into production. The organization's customers need to be maintained in order to maintain a revenue stream. Once the vital systems are restored, personnel can begin the second phase of recovery—the restoration of secondary systems and processes. Recovery and the resumption of operations are discussed in Section V.

In today's competitive environment, any business, industry, or government

DISASTER SNAPSHOT

The city archive in Cologne, Germany, collapsed on March 3, 2009, killing two men in a neighboring building and destroying about 15 percent of the historic documents housed in the archive. An investigation into the collapse revealed that a foreman of a crew working on the metro line going under the archive intentionally used fewer steel reinforcements at the site of the accident, selling the unused metal to scrap dealers, and falsifying the protocols for the work site.

The surviving documents, which date back as far as 1,000 years, were in varying states when rescue workers pulled them from the archive rubble, but less than one-quarter had been torn apart. Experts have since been working to piece them back together using software that was developed to restore shredded documents from the East German secret police, the Stasi.

Source: The Local, "Construction worker confesses in Cologne archive collapse case," *The Local: Germany's News in English,* 3 March 2009. 13 March 2011 <http://www.thelocal.de/article.php?ID=25131>.

organization must position itself to accept challenges that lie ahead. If a situation occurs that affects profitability or retained earnings, continued operation may be jeopardized. Planning is vital and necessary to mitigate losses. No organization can afford to lose customers because of failure to plan for and to manage disruptive events.

Business Continuity

Business continuity management (BCM) is a holistic management process that identifies potential impacts that threaten an organization and provides a framework for building resilience with the capability for an effective response that safeguards the interests of its key stakeholders, reputation, brand, and value creating activities.[10] To be successful, business continuity management must be fully integrated across the entire organization as a required management process. Business continuity management includes business continuity planning, which focuses mainly on incident response and, depending on the organization, can include records and information security and risk management processes.

A **business continuity plan (BCP)** is the documentation of a predetermined set of instructions or procedures that describe how an organization's business functions will be sustained during and after a significant disruption.[11]

Like emergency management, business continuity management relies on both critical business process identification and risk management results to determine the various priorities, tasks and procedures to include in the plans. While emergency management attempts to identify and mitigate all possible risks, business continuity management focuses on mitigating those risks that the organization cannot absorb—the risk tolerance of an organization. Risk tolerance is discussed more thoroughly in Chapter 3.

Benefits of Emergency Management and Business Continuity Planning

Comprehensive emergency management and business continuity planning yields many benefits for an organization's records, information, and assets if an emergency event occurs.

Stakeholders in the organization can gain comfort by knowing that measures have been taken to protect the organization from loss. Emergency management and business continuity planning includes the following benefits.

1. *Quick resumption of operations.* When an organization's personnel establish a plan, train personnel, complete preparedness activities, and test the plan, they are ready to handle a disruptive event. Even more important, if an event occurs, it has a good chance of being controlled so that it does not turn into a records and information disaster. These efforts result in the ability to maintain or resume normal operations quickly.

   Quick resumption of operations leads to continued profitability or revenue flow. An effective plan gives an organization the ability to successfully respond quickly to any major disruption that threatens its survival. Quick resumption of operations adds value to an organization and the products and services it delivers.

2. *Improved safety.* The courts could hold an organization negligent for not having a plan when an event caused an injury or took an employee's life. Material and supplies can be replaced; personnel are not recoverable. The U.S. Occupational Safety and Health Administration (OSHA) requires all employers to develop and implement an emergency action plan that includes protection procedures for personnel during and after an emergency.[12]

   The emergency management or business continuity plan should address key activities, such as training and risk mitigation, that will help keep people safe. Training provides the necessary knowledge to allow people to act safely and effectively. It also takes the surprise out of response activities. When an organization carries out training programs, personnel are more likely to behave appropriately in an emergency situation.

3. *Vital asset protection.* Emergency and business continuity management includes plans for protecting the organization's vital assets. The plan protects shareholders' investments, secures employees' jobs and retirement benefits, safeguards research, protects personal information, and maintains customer confidence and trust. Immediate resumption of operations and protection of personnel provide understandable benefits in addition to protecting material assets. For example, personnel can safeguard facilities, products, fleets, equipment, and furnishings during a disruptive event. However, without proper planning, the loss of any one of these assets will cause severe problems for the organization.

4. *Reduced insurance costs.* An emergency management or business continuity plan is a close partner of business insurance and security. Inadequate insurance and security can be ineffective and costly. The plan contains specific information about assets and risks, low cost preventive measures, and the cost of each protection program (such as a computer hot site, offsite records storage, or back-up hardware). Additionally, the plan contains schedules for periodic facility inspections and personnel training.

   Well-designed and maintained emergency management and business continuity plans can translate into premium reductions for specific types of business insurance. Organizations can reduce other types of insurance in addition to premium reductions through improved security, maintenance, and training programs. If an emergency management or business continuity plan is in place, an organization may reduce business resumption insurance and records restoration insurance costs that are portions of a total insurance package.

5. *Improved security.* The process of preparing an emergency management or business continuity plan includes a review of present security procedures to protect organizational facilities, personnel, records, and information from theft or acts of vandalism or terrorism. For example, the plan should include detailed procedures to monitor and control access to the facilities and equipment that contain vital records and information. Security is an important part of the mitigation phase of emergency or business continuity management.

6. *Legal compliance.* Organizations have defined legal responsibilities toward their shareholders, employees, government agencies, citizens, and customers. These responsibilities include taking reasonable measures to protect the organizations' assets, including records and information, and to remain in compliance with laws and regulations. Laws and regulations require emergency management or business continuity capabilities in several ways.

   • A specific *law* or *regulation* requires an organization to have an emergency management or business continuity plan.

   • A *contract* or *agreement* may require an organization to have a plan.

   • Legal precedent, as set by court cases, determine that organizations must have an established emergency management or business continuity plan.

   • A law or regulation may require compliance in such a way that protection from loss of records and information is implied.

7. *Reduction of errors from shock factor.* Without a plan, people will react haphazardly to a disruptive event. Some people may make mistakes due to insufficient or incorrect information, and some may freeze with fear and not react at all. Emergency management and business continuity plans are valuable tools in reducing the initial shock of a negative event.

   Emergency response planning exercises or mock drills place people in "what if" situations that increase awareness of how to behave in real events. People can reduce their fear and stress if they know what is expected of them. If an organization trains its employees and provides a plan for them to read and understand, they will behave • more effectively.

The organization's emergency management and business continuity plans should address all four phases of emergency management—*mitigation, preparedness, response,* and *recovery.* The organization that has developed comprehensive emergency management and BC plans will benefit greatly.

Records and Information Management Practices

Five elements of records and information management impact an effective emergency management or business continuity plan. (These elements are generally accepted practices. Some organizations may not implement all aspects of the elements due to resource constraints.)

1. Consider information as a critical resource throughout the organization.

2. Establish and maintain a current records and information inventory, an information systems inventory, and an inventory of electronically stored information (ESI).

3. Establish and maintain a documented records classification and retrieval system throughout the organization.

4. Establish and maintain documented records retention and disposition policies and procedures for the entire organization.

5. Develop and distribute a records management manual that includes all records and information management policies and procedures.

Information Viewed as a Resource

In most organizations critical resources receive the most support for mitigation and recovery efforts. Many organizations, however, do not always consider the records and information that are a part of the business processes of a critical resource. The growth of electronic recordkeeping systems as a basic business convention justifies the identification of information holdings as essential resources. Electronic records and data are essential tools in most business processes.

Statutory and regulatory requirements place a responsibility on the organization to identify and safeguard records and information necessary to show legal compliance, fiscal compliance, and to protect personal privacy. Security of these data and information should be part of emergency management or business continuity plans.

Some records and information are necessary during an event, and many are necessary afterwards for recovery. The administrative elements of emergency response include requirements for the creation and maintenance of certain essential records during an event. These records document response actions taken, the timeline of response actions, accounting for fund expenditures, documentation of any injuries sustained during response, and damage assessment records as the event progresses.

Records needed for damage financial recovery should also be considered a resource by the organization. Insurance companies will want damage documented, including "before" and "after" factors such as ownership, condition, cost, and so on. According to one director with the U.S. Federal Emergency Management Agency's (FEMA) Infrastructure Branch, "The most important thing for applicants [for FEMA's disaster recovery funding] is to be able to provide FEMA with a clear and complete view of their damages, the work they performed or will perform, and the costs they incurred." "The easiest way to do this is by having accurate and complete records."[13]

Records Inventory and ESI

To implement a successful plan to identify and protect records, organizations need to review the process of creating, arranging, storing, and retrieving records and information. A **record** is "recorded information, regardless of medium or characteristics, made or received by an organization in pursuance of legal obligations or in the transaction of business."[14] Information is recorded in many formats. Paper, microfilm, photographs, a variety of magnetic media, optical disks, audio tapes, and video recordings are all used as original media for creating, using, storing, and/or retrieving information. In addition, electronic records and data can be structured data sets, like databases; semistructured applications, like word processing files, email, and scanned images; and unstructured repositories, like file servers.

Data on the function, media or format type, and use of records and information collected on the records inventory are very useful to emergency management or business continuity planning. Data aid in determining records and information location and vulnerabilities and in identifying any existing protection. The inventory of existing records and information also aids in identifying and protecting vital records. An electronically stored information (ESI) data map for all electronic records can be used to identify electronic records and data that may have been damaged or lost. The map should include the custodian of the record, which electronic systems and formats are used to store the records or data, any limitations to accessibility of the records, and the retention policies for the records and data. Recovering records or data with expired retention is not economically feasible.

Documented Records Classification and Retrieval System

Lost or misfiled records and information can result in serious legal and monetary losses for an organization. Poorly organized files and inadequate labeling and indexing make finding records and information time-consuming and increases the likelihood of misfiling a record. These consequences are as true for electronic files as they are for paper files. Unorganized documents on diskettes, CDs, DVDs, hard drives, flash drives, external hard drives, or back-up tapes result in very time-consuming searches. Poorly labeled or named electronic files result in lost (unable to be retrieved) records.

Organized and well-indexed records are essential to timely and efficient resumption of operations following a disruptive event. Disorganized records and information significantly increase the cost of the recovery phase of emergency or business continuity management. Unorganized or poorly indexed records and information are nightmares to salvage or recreate from other sources. Documented indices and classification and retrieval systems help speed the re-creation of records from backups and other sources when necessary.

Documented Records Retention and Disposition Policy and Procedures

Records retention schedules, file plans, and records destruction policies are established to satisfy legal, audit, and business need requirements. Records management policies and procedures can be organized in a records management manual that should also include the emergency management or business continuity plan for records and information.

Without some type of established records management program, organizations leave themselves open to detrimental results. An organization can suffer fines, loss of legal rights, loss of revenue and profit, and uncollectable receipts. Sometimes, litigation can be lost because the lack of a records and information management retention and disposition program is interpreted as willful destruction of evidence. To protect the organization, policies and procedures should be in place to track all records destroyed. This tracking includes records destroyed during a disaster or during records salvage attempts following a disaster.

The records retention schedule helps identify *vital* or *mission-critical records*—records essential to critical business processes. **Critical business processes** are those parts or elements of an organization that are vital to everyday operations. If these critical processes are not performed, the organization may lose revenue and profits, experience increased operating costs following recovery, and possibly lose customers. The records retention schedule aids in indicating records of immediate value and priority during an emergency. A schedule also can function as a tool for pinpointing records and information that should exist and, therefore, must be found and recovered. Protecting records without knowing location, media, methods of protection, and the value of individual records is difficult. Without a records retention schedule and

QUICK TIPS

• Lists of file folder labels or word processing document names can function as file indexes.

• Every organization needs some form of a records retention schedule. Many professional organizations and records storage companies have sample business records retention schedules that can be adapted to any small organization's general business records.

• A one-page statement adopted by the board of directors or governing commission can be considered a records disposition policy.

organization file plan, reconstruction and salvage from a disorganized body of records and information will be very costly.

Emergency Management and Business Continuity for Records and Information

An emergency management or business continuity plan can be a significant catalyst for improving a records management program. The plan combines records management, information systems, telecommunications, and archival functions under a single, comprehensive program.

Where possible, the records and information emergency management or business continuity plan should also be a part of the overall organizational emergency management or business continuity program. In organizations where no comprehensive plan exists, the records and information plan must cover more criteria. These criteria may include requiring facility improvements or eliminating vulnerabilities. It may also include planning communications links and operations centers to restore access to records during a natural disaster.

Remember that recovery of records and information is only a small part of emergency management or business continuity plans. Safety of individuals will always take precedence over recovery of records and information, and the reestablishment of critical business processes will have priority.

An **emergency management or business continuity plan for records and information** is an approved, written, implemented, and periodically tested program to identify, protect, and reconstruct/salvage an organization's vital records and to establish procedures for the immediate resumption of business operations in case of a disaster. It is a dynamic, changing document requiring ongoing review and improvement. An emergency management or business continuity plan for records and information is used to:

- Identify mitigation measures against the loss of records and information.

- Identify alternative sources of the organization's records and information.

- Provide the basis for a systematic response to disruptive events that threaten an organization's records and information.

- Identify emergency response personnel and their roles.

- Establish procedures for recovery of damaged records and information.

- Establish recovery priorities.

- Identify sources of supplies, equipment, and services for recovery and restoration of damaged records and media.

New information technologies make records and information emergency management or business continuity planning more challenging and more complex. Records are created and stored on a variety of media and each of these different media requires some specific loss prevention and recovery techniques. Procedures for protecting and reconstructing information stored on magnetic media differ from those for protecting and salvaging information contained on paper records. A piece of paper can usually be quickly and easily dried after a flood, but a computer disk or tape needs technical expertise, and immediate, knowledgeable action to preserve the information it contains. Plans must include and provide for all media on which records are created and stored.

The type of physical damage to the records will determine the salvage methods necessary to recover the information. Fire-damaged records, particularly film and magnetic media, are often difficult to salvage. Vital records lost through theft, misfiling, or data entry error must often be reconstructed from designated back-up copies. Water-damaged records are the most frequent objects of salvage efforts and form the center of many records and information emergency management and business continuity plans.

An emergency management or business continuity plan for records and information has four objectives:

1. *Mitigation.* Identify and adequately protect the organization's vital records and information.

2. *Preparedness.* Reduce the risk of disasters caused by human error, deliberate destructiveness, building/equipment failure or malfunction, and the adverse consequences of all disasters by mandating specific security, maintenance, and training programs; establishing vital records programs; planning response strategies; and by explaining policies, procedures, and resources to be activated in emergency situations.

3. *Response.* Ensure the organization's ability to continue or resume operations effectively after a major event by activating the response plan and setting in place planned alternative operating procedures and locations.

4. *Recovery.* Ensure the organization's ability to recover lost or endangered information rapidly by reconstructing and/or salvaging damaged records after a major disaster. Establish detailed recovery procedures and a management structure to carry out these procedures.

The operational impact of a disruptive event is defined by the length of time it shuts down or interrupts an essential business process or organizational function. Where records and information can be restored or salvaged, the impact is usually confined to the period immediately following the event. Where records and information are lost or destroyed, the organization may be affected for many years.

A primary benefit of an emergency management or business continuity plan is rapid resumption of operations or services. The technological atmosphere of most organizations requires immediate access to electronic information for most business processes. Plans should provide procedures for routine data backup, protective storage of back-up data, and alternative sites to ensure this access.

QUICK TIP

Emergencies for some small businesses can happen at any time, especially if the business is located adjacent to another business. Discussing the importance of emergency management principles and concepts with business neighbors can often prevent a records and information disaster.

Planning information protection can lead to improved information security. The need for physical security of records is widely recognized. Organizations do not always consider the need to protect internal information, particularly electronic data and records. Increasing use of Internet services, email, and social media can expose an organization to many information security problems. Patent or design information can be stolen, personal information can be compromised, computers can be exposed to viruses, and unwise email conversations can become legally embarrassing.

Protection of records is essential to meet statutory and regulatory requirements. If a regulatory authority requires accounting records to be produced during an audit, those records must be protected against loss. Records required by litigation must be produced or accounted for even if the organization was put out of business by a disaster. Records and data containing personal information must be secured. In the United States, the Internal Revenue Service holds officers and directors responsible for creating and maintaining organization records. The Foreign Corrupt Practices Law holds specific officers and directors of some organizations liable for negligence when they fail to take reasonable precautions to protect an organization's records. The Office of the Comptroller of the Currency requires officers of nationally chartered banks to review their contingency plans annually. Almost every state has legislation setting the required procedures for responding to a breach of personal data.

Emergency management and business continuity planning can improve information systems operations. Planning protection and recovery procedures will show any deficiencies in hardware and software compatibility and accessibility, comprehensive information and system security programs, comprehensive and consistent data backup, data back-up storage and recovery procedures, and cross-training on using software and database programs.

Some elements of a plan may be fully in place before the planning process begins; some may only be in an elementary stage. A plan can be a powerful stimulus for enhancing security, viewing improved management of information as essential to a company's survival, and establishing more effective methods for managing all company information. Establishing and using the plan can make the difference between inconvenience or slight delay and catastrophic loss.

A solid emergency management or business continuity plan for records and information can improve the response to requirements of the overall organization plan. Information accessed quickly and accurately during a disruptive event or immediately following an event greatly increases the speed of resumption of operations.

"In the wake of the 9/11 terrorist attack, one brokerage firm stood out in terms of IT Disaster Recovery: Cantor Fitzgerald. Its office was located in the World Trade Center towers in New York City and was seriously affected in terms of lives and data lost. Yet, within a few days of the disaster, Cantor Fitzgerald was believed to be operational in another location, having recovered much of the information lost due to a well-planned IT Disaster Recovery Plan (DRP)."[15]

Lesson Learned

"The continued operations of an organization depend on management's awareness of potential disasters, their ability to develop a plan to minimize disruptions of critical functions and the capability to recover operations expediently and successfully."[16]

CHAPTER 1 CHECKLIST

Emergency Management Concepts

☐ Know and understand the difference between a records and information "emergency" and a "disaster."

☐ Know and understand the four phases of emergency management: mitigation, preparedness, response, and recovery.

☐ Know and understand the benefits of emergency management planning:

    ☐ Quick resumption of operations

    ☐ Improved safety

    ☐ Protection of vital assets

    ☐ Reduced insurance costs

    ☐ Improved security

    ☐ Legal compliance

    ☐ Reduction of errors from shock factor

Records and Information Management Practices

☐ Consider information as a critical resource throughout the organization.

☐ Establish and maintain a current records and information inventory and a current ESI map.

☐ Establish and maintain a documented records and information classification and retrieval system throughout the organization.

☐ Establish and maintain documented records retention and disposition policies and procedures for the entire organization.

☐ Develop and distribute a records management manual that includes all records and information management policies and procedures. At a minimum, this manual should include a records retention schedule, documented file systems, an emergency response plan, and records disposition policy and procedures.

Emergency Management for Records and Information

☐ Understand the objectives of an emergency management or business continuity plan for records and information.

☐ Identify all records media and understand the protection and recovery methods necessary to safeguard each type of records media.

☐ Determine any statutory and regulatory requirements for the protection of the organization's records.

☐ Determine any elements of the plan that may already exist within the organization.

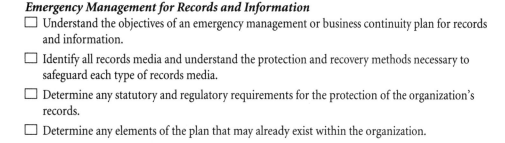

NOTES

1. Michael Wallace and Lawrence Webber, *The Disaster Recovery Handbook: A Step-by-Step Plan to Ensure Business Continuity and Protect Vital Operations, Facilities and Assets* (New York: AMACOM, 2004), xi.

2. Jeffrey B. Bumgarner, *Emergency Management* (California: ABC CLIO, Inc., 2008), 13.

3. Bumgarner, *Emergency Management*, 13.

4. "Some Common Fire Cause," *Fire Safety Fundamentals*, vol. 3 (n.p.: Factory Mutual Systems, n.d.), 2.

5. Bumgarner, *Emergency Management*, 17.

6. Rae Zimmerman, "The Relationship of Emergency Management to Governmental Policies on Man-Made Technological Disasters," *Public Administration Review* 45, special issue January 1985): 37.

7. David McLoughlin, "A Framework for Integrated Emergency Management," *Public Administration Review* 45, special issue (January 1985): 166.

8. McLoughlin, "A Framework for Integrated Emergency Management,"166.

9. McLoughlin, "A Framework for Integrated Emergency Management,"166.

10. Ian Charters FBCI, *A Management Guide to Implementing Global Good Practice in Business Continuity Management, Section 1: BCM Policy & Programme Management* (Business Continuity Institute, United Kingdom: 2008), 5.

11. National Institute of Standards and Technology, SP800-34, *Contingency Planning Guide for Information Technology Systems* (June 2002), D-4.

12. U.S. Code of Federal Regulations §1917.30.

13. Federal Emergency Management Agency, "Good Record Keeping Speeds Local Disaster Recovery," FEMA media release number: 1850-004, Release Date: August 4, 2009.

14. ARMA International, *Glossary of Records and Information Management Terms*, 3rd ed., (Prairie Village, KS: ARMA International, 2007), 20.

15. Krishna Chandler, "Disaster Recovery – Lessons Learned from the Hurricanes," *EMS Newsletter* (October 18, 2005).

16. Wallace and Webber, *The Disaster Recovery Handbook*, xi.

Preparing an Emergency Management Plan: Initial Steps

"...the most convincing reason for having a business continuity plan is that it simply makes good business sense to have a company protected from a major disaster."[1]

Gain Top Management Support

To prepare for, respond to, and recover from a disruptive event effectively, the organizational culture must first recognize that the organization is susceptible to some catastrophe. Because an investment of resources is required to develop and sustain an emergency management or business continuity plan, support for the plan from top management must be in place from the beginning. Time, funding, sometimes equipment and supplies, occasionally physical adjustments to facilities, and changes to business processes may be necessary to prevent an emergency from becoming a disaster. Top managers and employees must support the concept of emergency management and business continuity before a plan can be developed.

Prepare Emergency Management Proposal

Ideally, embedding acceptance of emergency management or business continuity management into the organizational culture is easier if the concept originates from the top of the organizational hierarchy. However, lower level managers and employees often initiate the need for and accept responsibility for an emergency management or business continuity plan. A safety officer, chief information officer (CIO), emergency response coordinator, records and information management professional, or facility maintenance manager may be the plan developer.

A successful plan is often developed by a team consisting of representatives of various organizational functions including:

- Emergency management director
- Procurement officer
- Financial manager
- Safety officer
- Information technology manager or CIO
- Records manager
- Facility manager
- Operations manager
- Human resources manager

The plan should be considered a priority project that is supported by a memorandum or policy. The team should prepare and present to management a proposal for allocating resources necessary to develop the plan.[2] The proposal should provide basic costs and benefits associated with having a plan. Prepare a formal cost-benefit analysis or simply include anticipated costs and benefits to the organization in the proposal narrative. The proposal should also include a summary business impact assessment or a vulnerability assessment, whichever is commonly used in the organization.

Although most organizational management determines the allocation of resources for implementing a plan based on financial considerations, the goal of developing an emergency management or business continuity plan is to protect lives and the future of the organization. Therefore, the cost-benefit analysis and BIA should provide enough information for a management decision with the understanding that the initial analyses are not comprehensive.

Another tool that may aid in gaining top management support for emergency management or business continuity planning is a vulnerability assessment. A **vulnerability assessment** is the process of identifying, quantifying, and prioritizing (or ranking) the vulnerabilities in a system such as nuclear power plants, information technology systems, energy supply systems, water supply systems, transportation systems, and communication systems. In emergency and business continuity management, it means assessing the threats from potential hazards to the population and to the infrastructure for that particular system.[3] Vulnerability assessments are discussed in more detail in Chapter 3.

Organizational management may want to consider outsourcing plan development to an emergency management or business continuity professional firm rather than develop the plan with in-house resources. Use of an external consultant may require more cost to provide time for the consultant to get to know the organization. If outsourcing is chosen, then a major consideration for the organization is how detailed to develop specifications for the plan. The *extent* of the specifications will determine the cost of the contract. If specifications are vague, a poor and ineffective plan will result. Specifications and plan requirements that are too detailed can result in a high cost for plan development.

Use of in-house resources to develop a plan is often less costly than outsourcing, if enough in-house expertise is available to accomplish the tasks. This book is organized to assist plan development with in-house resources.

QUICK TIP

The small business owner can and will make the decision to develop an emergency management plan. He or she may decide to do it on the basic merits and common sense of having a plan, or to conduct a survey with other business owners to see what actions they have taken.

A good way to get help is to visit the local emergency management coordinator who will be more than happy to work with the small business owner to ensure that a plan is developed.

Perform Cost-Benefit Analysis

A **cost-benefit analysis** is a management tool to aid in decision-making.[4] It is the process of gathering information, analyzing the data, and subsequently documenting the results to determine costs and benefits of a program. Good research showing start-up and ongoing costs and expected benefits of a new or existing program can assist management in deciding whether to proceed with the plan. To be successful, the proposal must have information that management can use to decide for or against the allocation of resources.

Not all benefits can be quantified. The key is to state the major benefits that can result from plan development. Potential benefits may include:

- Continuation of service or operations without loss of revenue
- Compliance with federal, state, or local laws and regulations
- Health and safety of customers, employees, and vendors
- Customer satisfaction through goodwill and credibility
- Continuation of communication and information flow

Stating benefits as negatives may be helpful. For example, instead of stating, "the organization can continue operations and revenue flow," state, "failure to develop a plan may result in the discontinuance of operations and cash flow." Use the negative approach cautiously. A negative statement often invokes questions of how and why. Be prepared to support negative statements.

Listing quantifiable costs will improve the chances for gaining management support for the plan. Management will want to know potential costs associated with plan research and development. Other cost considerations include:

- Corrections or modifications to facilities or processes due to the results of the risk management process and/or vulnerability assessment
- Changes to business processes to prevent loss
- Human resources expenditures for plan research and development
- Materials and supplies for documenting and recording the plan
- Equipment and supplies for emergency preparedness activities
- Training

Format the cost-benefit analysis document in simple, understandable terms. State (briefly) the key benefits and associated costs. Address the issue of payback, or the overall cost-justification for plan development, with care. **Payback** is that point in time when an organization's investment, or cash flow, is returned in the form of benefit. Emergency management requires an initial outlay of funding and investment into ensuring that the organization is prepared for a disruptive event. Obviously, resources will be needed to research, plan, develop, and carry out a thorough emergency management or business continuity plan for records and information. The organization will not realize a payback until an event triggers the activation of the plan. If the event occurs and the plan helps to reduce loss successfully, only then will payback be realized. However, the ideal plan will include tactics to prevent as much loss as possible, and will, therefore, make quantifiable payback difficult to calculate. The advantage of a good plan will be intangible benefits such as those listed in the previous paragraph. Chapter 6 addresses the issue of payback in more detail and discusses specific budget considerations.

Understand the Role of Business Impact Analysis

A **business impact analysis (BIA)** looks at critical processes and determines the impact on the organization if the process is interrupted. A summary BIA gives a big picture view of potential loss to the organization if an emergency management or business continuity plan is not in place. A full BIA is an important step in the risk mitigation process (discussed in Chapter 3). The strategy of this approach is to quantify the potential losses of an organization as the result of a disruptive event, and to research and present recommendations to reduce or mitigate these losses.

One of the most important aspects of the BIA is to determine which processes of the organization are essential to the continued operation both during and following a disruptive event. Each process is valued according to its critical worth to the organization. For example, the customer service processes of an organization may be essential and are placed back into operation immediately, while restoration of the accounting processes may be delayed a few days or up to a week.

The BIA identifies those business processes that must be resumed urgently and those that may be resumed later. It considers the operational, financial, and other impacts and exposures for each part of the organization if a serious disruption occurs. Lost revenue, for example, can affect cash flow that will be needed to meet normal operating expenses and recovery operations. Manufacturing work flow interruptions can affect quality control or compliance processes. As with the cost-benefit analysis, the BIA should also identify the minimum financial, human, and information resources needed to support the elements of the proposed plan.

Present Proposal to Management

Once the cost analysis or BIA is completed, the proposal for plan development is presented to top management. The entire development team, representing all major functions, should be part of the presentation. Begin the presentation by briefly explaining the logic behind those present at the meeting. Key managers that should attend the presentation include:

- President or chief executive officer
- Emergency management director
- Financial manager
- Safety officer
- Chief information officer
- Records manager
- Facility manager
- Operations manager
- Other appropriate employees

To develop and carry out a successful emergency management or business continuity plan will take many persons in the organization who support the idea of mitigation, preparedness, response, and recovery of essential business processes and their supporting records and information. Therefore, include the organizational personnel who will most likely be part of the team to develop and implement the plan.

Use an approach that will make this internal presentation match the organization's culture. Consider these recommendations:

- Keep it simple and understandable. Too much technical jargon and too many acronyms can result in negative reactions.
- State the purpose and scope of the plan development and implementation project and objectives that the organization will accomplish.
- Provide background for the project or cite some applicable case studies to support the initiative. Discuss benefits and associated costs.
- Recommend ways in which the project should continue.

Develop a Policy Statement

Once management approval to proceed is obtained, all personnel should be informed through a clearly defined policy stating that the plan is a part of the organizational culture and will be developed and implemented. A sample policy statement is shown in Figure 2.1. The policy statement can be a simple narrative that includes the following components:

1. Purpose of the emergency management or business continuity plan
2. Goals of the organization regarding emergency management or business continuity of essential business processes and their supporting records and information
3. Scope of the plan and functions in the organization to which it will apply
4. Elements of the plan and roles and responsibilities of persons responsible for each element
5. Organizational resources required to develop and implement the plan
6. Plan testing and personnel training requirements
7. The intent to review and maintain the plan once implemented

After the approving authority has signed the written policy and the policy is disseminated throughout the organization, subsequent steps for plan development and implementation can begin. By getting top managers involved from the onset, they will continue to support the plan as it is developed, implemented, and maintained.

Policy Statement

Effective Date: January 1, 2011

Subject: Records and Information Emergency Management Plan

I. Purpose

An emergency management [or business continuity] plan is established to provide guidance and procedures necessary to ensure that disruptive events are mitigated or eliminated and that the organization and its resources are protected.

II. Scope

This policy applies to all functions of the organization and, as such, all employees are expected to study and obtain a knowledge of the information contained herein.

All employees shall receive training on emergency management procedures.

III. Policy

The policy of this organization is to establish, maintain, and exercise a comprehensive emergency management plan to ensure that the protection of the organization and its resources and to assure return to critical operations following a disruptive event. Responsibility for plan development and implementation resides with the Emergency Management Officer, the Safety Director, the Chief Information Officer, and the Records Manager. The plan will be reviewed annually and revised as necessary.

This organization supports the team concept for plan development and all activities appropriate with the implementation of the plan. To be successful, all employees must understand the plan components and their role in carrying out the plan in the event of a disruptive event.

The following organizational assets shall take priority in plan development and implementation:

- All employees and stakeholders
- Facilities
- Vital records and information
- Equipment and furnishings

Approval: _____   Date: _____

Figure 2.1 Sample Policy Statement

Focus on Business Process Management

A key factor in a successful emergency management or business continuity plan is determining those business processes that are critical for the organization to remain in business following a disruptive event. This determination is best accomplished by defining **business processes** throughout the organization. A business process is a series of steps designed to produce a product or service.[5] Examples include the manufacture of a tire, the treatment of water, the sale of electricity to the regional grid, and developing or gaining approval for a new prescription drug. Avoid confusing a business process with a business function. Human resources, for example, is a business function that may include several processes such as recruiting staff, intake processing of a new hire, terminating an employee, and issuing paychecks.

Business process management (BPM) is the achievement of an organization's objectives through the improvement, management, and control of essential business processes.[6] Business process management must impact the organization by delivering benefits. It should focus on the core business processes that are essential to the primary business activity—those processes that contribute towards the achievement of the strategic objectives of the organization.[7] Once the core processes are identified, analysis of the role of each process in the organizational structure is necessary to determine which processes are critical to continued operations. BPM is also a significant tool for recognizing risk and

DISASTER SNAPSHOT

A Philadelphia city employee and three others were accused of selling more than 24,000 public records on the black market. A records clerk and three people who worked for businesses that needed incident, accident, and other reports faced federal charges after a records clerk allegedly copied records that would usually cost $20 to $25 and sold them for $5 each, pocketing almost $200,000 for herself. Over 24,000 reports were provided to these individuals. The clerk personally received over $185,000, which she kept. The city should have received $600,415 for those reports. The city is working to tighten records department accountability to prevent similar incidents.

Source: Upfront, "Philly Clerk Allegedly Sold City Records," *Information Management*, November/December 2010.

determining mitigation of risk to the organization, as discussed in Chapter 3.

BPM is the best way to determine which processes are essential. While analysis of the various business processes in the organization is generally a technique used to improve processes, it can also help define the processes that are critical for the organization to remain in business following a disruptive event. The processes for analysis are often depicted by a process flow diagram, which uses graphic elements to represent tasks, flows, and storage. A process flow diagram most often takes the form of a process flow chart. For records and information emergency management and business continuity purposes, the BPA should show not only the components, tasks, and flow of the process, but also the records, documents, data, and other information that support the process, which is important for vital records identification as discussed in Chapter 4. Figure 2.2 shows a sample flow diagram for a business process including identified supporting records and information.

The steps for defining an essential business process for emergency management or business continuity purposes can include:

1. Identify processes that meet strategic goals or core mission objectives of the organization.

2. Create a flow diagram for each process that breaks the process down into its major steps. Include records, documents, data, and other information that support the process or are created by the process.

3. Identify process gaps, missing steps, or subprocesses that would help meet strategic goals or core mission objectives.

4. Identify risks within the process that would result in loss to the organization.

5. Identify mitigation activities that would close process gaps and/or would reduce the identified risk.

6. Modify process design to incorporate mitigation.

7. Ensure that individuals responsible for the new process components and controls are identified in the process model.

8. Distribute the process design to subject matter experts for their input, feedback, and constructive criticism.

9. Make final adjustments to the design.

10. Implement approved process design.

"A survey of the state of preservation of cultural collections in the United States (the Heritage Health Index) indicated that 80% of libraries and archives in the western region and American Pacific were not prepared to respond to collection disasters. They did not have a written disaster response plan or a staff trained to carry it out."[8]

Lesson Learned

"The size of the disaster is not the determining factor of staying in business; it is the business continuity plan that will determine if the doors will stay open or be closed."[9]

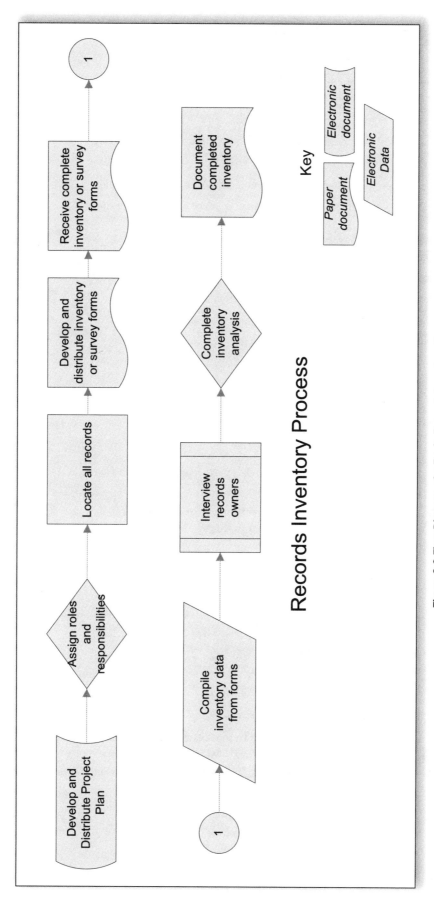

Figure 2.2 Flow Diagram of a Basic Records Inventory Process

CHAPTER 2 CHECKLIST

Gaining Top Management Support

- ☐ Prepare emergency management proposal.
- ☐ Assemble emergency management plan team.
- ☐ Conduct a cost-benefit analysis or business impact assessment.
- ☐ Develop the proposal.
- ☐ Present the proposal to top managers, team members, and other key employees.
- ☐ Develop a policy statement with management approval to validate their support.

Business Process Management

- ☐ Define essential business processes.
- ☐ Create a process flow diagram, including supporting records and information.
- ☐ Determine the processes that are critical for business continuity.
- ☐ Identify potential risk of loss exhibited in the work flow for each process.
- ☐ Identify mitigation steps to reduce the loss risk.

NOTES

1. Ken Doughty, *Business Continuity Planning: Protect Your Organization's Life* (CRC Press LLC, 2001), 7.

2. Geoffrey H. Wold, "The Disaster Recovery Planning Process: part I of III," *Disaster Recovery Journal* 5, no. 1 (January/February/March 1992): 29.

3. Wikipedia, 15 March 2011 <*http://en.wikipedia.org/wiki/Vulnerability_assessment*>.

4. David N. Ammons, *Administrative Analysis for Local Government: Practical Application of Selected Techniques* (Athens, GA: The University of Georgia, 1991), 93.

5. Geary A. Rummler and Alan P. Brache, *Improving Performance: How to manage the white space on the organizational chart* (San Francisco: Jossey-Bass, 1995). 15 March 2011 <*http://en.wikipedia.org/wiki/Business_process#cite_ref-2*>.

6. John Jeston and Johan Nelis, *Business Process Management, Practical Guidelines to Successful Implementations* (Oxford, U.K.: Elsevier, 2006), 11.

7. Jeston and Nelis, *Business Process Management,* 10.

8. Lynn Ann Davis, "Disaster October 2004: Lessons Learned from Flashflood at University of Hawaii at Manoa Library (Honolulu, Hawaii)," World Library and Information Congress: 72d IFLA General Conference and Council, 20-24 August 2006, Seoul, South Korea, 2.

9. Ken Doughty, *Business Continuity Planning,* 7.

SECTION II:
MITIGATION

The first phase in emergency management and business continuity is mitigation. **Mitigation** for records and information includes all activities that reduce the degree of long-term risk from natural and human hazards. Records and information mitigation has three parts—risk management processes, a vital records program, and a loss prevention plan. The risk management processes and the vital records program become a part of the loss prevention plan. The loss prevention plan, in turn, becomes a part of the emergency management or business continuity plan.

Risk Management

"Failing to manage risk is the corporate equivalent of a rabbit caught in the headlights of an oncoming vehicle—doing nothing can be dangerous."[1]

Risk is the exposure to the chance of injury or loss.[2] The cost of mitigating the risk of loss of records and information must be weighed against the value of the information to the organization. This evaluation is accomplished by determining the vulnerabilities of the records and by comparing all costs associated with the loss of the records and information against the cost of protecting or reconstructing the records. Because disasters result in significant financial and operational damage and loss, an organization must take preemptive measures to mitigate risk before a disaster can occur.

Identifying and mitigating all risk can be time consuming and costly. Some organizations may want to expend only the minimum resources to mitigate risk to one or more critical processes and accept the risk to the rest of the business. Other organizations may want to reduce as much risk as possible, no matter the cost. To achieve a cost and resource balance in risk mitigation, the organization must set its risk tolerance level. The **risk tolerance level** is the maximum exposure to risk, whether for a given type of risk or across all exposures, that is acceptable based on the benefits and costs involved.[3] Risk tolerance should align with the strategic goals of the organization. The organization should link its risk tolerance and risk objectives to its business goals and objectives.[4]

Risk management is the culture, processes, and structures that are put into place to effectively manage potential negative events. As eliminating all risk is not possible, the objective of risk management is to reduce risks to an acceptable level.[5] Risk management is used to identify vulnerabilities and hazards that should be mitigated and to calculate the cost of mitigation and recovery. Therefore, risk management is necessary for development of a meaningful records and information mitigation, preparedness, response, and recovery program.

Andrew Holmes, author of *Risk Management*, has opted to categorize risk based upon its impact to the organization. His classification scheme is comprised of five risks:[6]

1. Strategic risk (impacts the organization's strategic direction)

2. Business/Financial risk (impacts the organization financially)

3. Program and project risk (impacts success of change initiatives)

4. Operational risk (impacts overall business operations)

5. Technological risk (impacts success of new technology)

The Records and Information Risk Management Maturity Model, as outlined by risk management experts Michel Crouhy, Dan Galai, and Robert Market, identifies five stages necessary for an effective records and information risk management program.[7]

1. *Ad hoc stage.* Risks are addressed through other business processes, focusing primarily on loss avoidance.

2. *Awareness.* The organization recognizes the need to focus on records and information risk management as a unique, separate element.

3. *Monitoring.* Internal risk factors are tracked at the business unit level (records management, IT, legal, etc.).

4. *Formalizing.* Organization incorporates records and information risk management, as a unit, into its documented risk management policies and procedures.

5. *Mature.* Organization has fully integrated its records and information risk management unit into its comprehensive risk management program.

Risk management includes risk assessment, risk analysis, and business impact analysis processes. Applying these processes to emergency or business continuity planning is necessary to produce an adequate, cost-effective records and information emergency management or business continuity program. Risk management for records and information includes a number of factors—loss or damage vulnerability, information security, privacy protection, and legal compliance. It should include the management of all potential risk, including physical risk, legal risk, privacy protection risk, and data and information security risk. Figure 3.1 shows a records and information risk management flow model.

Records and Information Risk Management Flow Model

Business Process Analysis
- Identify and conduct a process analysis for each business process.
- Identify records and information that support each process.
- Identify critical business processes.
- Align RIM processes to reflect and support the overall business strategy where necessary.

Risk Management Process
- Apply risk management processes to each business process.
- Assess existing risk management and assess records and information management risk controls.
- Include all potential risk.
  — Physical risks
  — Legal risks
  — Privacy protection risks
  — Data and information security risks
- Complete the risk management cycle.
  — Set strategic goals, objectives, and constraints.
  — Evaluate alternatives.
  — Determine and implement risk action—accept and monitor the risk, accept and change the risk tolerance, mitigate the risk.
  — Implement and monitor.
- Complete risk management processes for identified records and information risk.
  — Records risk assessment
  — Records risk analysis
  — Business impact analysis
- Develop organization emergency management or business continuity plan.
- Develop vital records program (see separate flow, Chapter 4).
- Develop and implement loss prevention plan (see Chapter 5).
- Establish and implement records and information audit program.

Figure 3.1 Records and Information Risk Management Flow Model

Risk Assessment

Risk assessment looks at *existing* risk to records and information. Such risks vary, ranging from those typically addressed by emergency management or business continuity programs—damage to or loss of records and information arising from disasters or major system faults, for example—to more systemic problems with records and information.[8]

The risk assessment process involves:

- Evaluating existing physical and environmental security and controls and assessing their adequacy relative to potential threats to records and information;

- Conducting a physical site survey to determine where security and controls exist and where potential hazards to records and information exist;

- Identifying and recommending new or improved security and controls to protect records and information; and

- Establishing security and controls to protect identified vital records and information.[9]

A portion of a sample risk assessment is shown in Figure 3.2.

Facility	Risks	Vulnerabilities
Plant 1	• Fire • Equipment malfunction • Water damage • Flood • Personal injury • Electronic data loss • Inaccessible due to radiation leak	• No equipment safety program • Old building – does not meet current codes • Increased equipment downtime over past year • Building on flood plain of XYZ River • Building 10 miles from Nuclear Power Plant

Figure 3.2 A Portion of a Risk Assessment

A successful risk assessment is dependent upon a defined course of action. Consistent terminology, driven by pre-established definitions and concepts, is critical. This consistency, best achieved by utilizing classification schemes, must be established prior to the commencement of the risk assessment task.

Promoted by records and information specialist Victoria Lemieux, an *Effectiveness Rating* can be used to calculate the effectiveness of current records and information controls. An *Effectiveness Rating Formula*, cited below, is used to determine the effectiveness of the controls for a given record or information.[10]

Sum of Quality Rankings – Sum of Satisfaction Rankings = Effectiveness Rating

This calculation is dependent upon the identification and ranking of the quality of records critical to business processes (the type of records and information required to complete the transactions of the process effectively and to meet accountabilities), coupled with the identification and evaluation of gaps between records requirements and the degree to which existing systems satisfy these requirements.

Begin by identifying and ranking each quality characteristic. Then, rank the level of satisfaction obtained from each characteristic and perform the calculation. For example, importance can be ranked on a scale of 1 to 4 (with four being the highest existing quality), and satisfaction can be ranked on the same scale (with four being the highest level of existing satisfaction).

Quality Characteristic	Quality Importance	Level of Satisfaction
Accuracy	3	3
Authenticity	3	2
Retrievability	2	1

The total of the satisfaction ratings are subtracted from the total of the quality ratings to indicate the effectiveness of the program. The higher the effectiveness rating, the less effective the existing risk control for records and information.

Sum of Quality Rankings minus **Sum of Satisfaction Ranking** = **Effectiveness Rating**
(3 + 3 + 2 = 8)   minus   (3 + 2 + 1 = 6)   =   (8 – 6 = 2)

The effectiveness rating can be used to prioritize identified records and information risks and to quantify the need for mitigating those risks.

Changes required for risk reduction may not necessitate improving or changing records control mechanisms. Instead, it may necessitate changes or enhancements to *business function* controls within the business process.

Vulnerability assessment has many things in common with risk assessment. Assessments are typically performed according to the following steps:

1. Catalog assets and capabilities (resources) in a system.

2. Assign quantifiable value (or at least rank order) and importance to those resources.

3. Identify the vulnerabilities or potential threats to each resource.

4. Mitigate or eliminate the most serious vulnerabilities for the most valuable resources.

In the United States, guides that provide valuable considerations and templates for completing a vulnerability assessment are available from numerous agencies, including the Department of Energy, the Environmental Protection Agency, and the United States Department of Transportation.

Site Survey

Conducting an onsite survey of all organizational facilities and storage areas is the best way to identify potential problems. A **site survey** is a review of a facility or location in which hazards or vulnerabilities such as leaky roofs, fire hazards, lack of fire suppression, and insect infestation are documented. A site survey includes:

- Geographic location of all offices and facilities

- Knowledge and understanding of the business processes and supporting records and information

- Location of all physical records and information, including enclosures, housing, and storage environment

- Existence and purpose of all electronic records and information systems

- Current potential hazards to records and information

- Type of structure and safety environment

- Specific areas of vulnerability

- Current alternative protection for vulnerable records and information

Some vulnerabilities come from the geographic location of the facility. In addition to the potential damage from natural events, the facility may be located near the sources of possible radiation leaks, hazardous waste spills, chemical explosions, train derailments, or airplane crashes. Some electronic records and information are vulnerable to security violations, either jeopardizing the continued operation of the electronic systems or breaching secured personal or business confidential information.

During the survey, the following items should be identified, recognized, documented, and, in some cases, investigated:

- Vital records, their location, and method of storage

- All information and communication equipment, types, location, use, serial numbers, and vendors

- Any records containing personal or confidential information
- Dangerous storage practices that increase the risk of fire or water damage
- All potential electronic system security vulnerabilities
- The proximity of water and sewer pipes, windows, electrical wiring and outlets, and heating/air-conditioning equipment
- Unsafe or unwise use of potentially hazardous tools and equipment
- Potential exposure of computers or computer networks to computer viruses or personal data breaches
- Key fire hazards—electrical defects, incendiaries, smoking, and combustibles in contact with hot surfaces such as drapes or curtains resting against space heaters[11]
- Evidence of leaking gas lines, leaking roofs or windows, faulty electrical wiring, or insect or rodent presence
- Existing security devices that prevent or detect unauthorized access to records and information
- Inspection records for heating, ventilation, and air conditioning (HVAC) systems, and other mechanical equipment

Determine whether the facility structure and safety environment includes the risk of human disasters. Some items to consider: type of building, fire and security alarms, fire suppression systems, availability and location of fire extinguishers, overall condition of the building, location of fire hydrants, and the proximity of lakes, rivers, or reservoirs.

A sample site survey form is shown in Figures 3.3a and 3.3b.

A general security program for both facilities and information provides a necessary framework within which a records and information emergency management or business continuity plan can be developed. Elements of an existing security program are interwoven throughout the fabric of an emergency management or business continuity plan. Computer passwords; employee identification cards; data encryption; security guards; restricted access areas; duplicate microforms; replicated data systems; fire resistant vaults and safes; smoke, water, and fire detectors; offsite records storage areas; and burglar alarms are a few of the long list of security measures commonly found in businesses.

The following eight basic steps should be taken to ensure that information remains secure.

1. Determine the information to be protected.

2. Identify individuals who create, transmit, receive, and distribute sensitive information.

3. Define ways in which personally identifiable or confidential information is handled.

4. Define clear-cut procedures for the protection of personally identifiable or confidential information.

5. Provide prompt access to needed information.

6. Balance the need for security against the need for operational effectiveness.

7. Develop detailed procedures and assign responsibility.

8. Develop employee training programs.[12]

Electronic records are very vulnerable to data loss. Electrical surges or voltage drops can play havoc with electronic systems. Magnetic tapes are susceptible to loss of data if they are exposed to strong magnetic fields or elevated temperature and humidity conditions. Electronic data networks are threatened by computer viruses, data breaches, software and hardware incompatibilities, and human error or incompetence.

Software can be destroyed or damaged, leaving it unavailable for restoration. Protection of electronic systems must include backup of all operating system programs and all software applications. When

Records and Information Risk Assessment
Site Survey

Date: _03/07/2011_   Surveyor: _Jane Doe_

Place:
Facility: _Plant 1_   Room: _Accounting Office_

Location in Building: _northwest corner_

Type of Building: _brick, 2-story_

Roof Type & Condition: _sloped, asphalt shingles, good condition_

Approx. Room Size: _15' x 25'_

Windows/Doors: _1 interior door, 4 exterior windows_

Loft or Mezzanine Storage: [X] Yes   [ ] No

Locality Risk: _building 5' from reservoir_

Climate:
High/Low Temperature Range: _70° - 90°_

Heating: [ ] Yes   [X] No

Air-Conditioning: [ ] Yes   [X] No

Humidity Control: [ ] Yes   [X] No

Temperature/Humidity Monitoring: [ ] Yes   [X] No

Lighting:
[X] Natural   [ ] Fluorescent   [ ] UV Control

[ ] Incandescent   [X] Direct Sunlight: _near windows_

Security:
Entry Alarms: [ ] Doors   [ ] Windows   [ ] Motion Sensors

Fire Alarms: [X] Heat   [ ] Smoke

Automatic Extinguishers: _none_

Type: _____   Location: _____

Portable Extinguishers: _2_

Type: _ABC, chemical foam_   Location: _1 in office, 1 in hall near office door_

Insurance: _liability, physical property damage_

Vulnerabilities:
Fire: _____

Electrical: _does not meet current code_   Heating: _does not meet current code_

Equipment: _no safety program, frequent downtime_

Water: _____

Plumbing: _does not meet current code, restrooms and small kitchen near office_

Moisture Accumulation: _none apparent_

Building Leaks: _ceiling, around all external windows_

Evidence of: [ ] Insects   [ ] Rodents   [X] Humidity Extremes   [ ] Temperature Extremes   [X] Mold/Mildew

Other: _____

_____

_____

Figure 3.3a Site Survey (Page 1)

Records and Information Risk Assessment
Site Survey (continued)

Records/Information Housing:

Record (1): _Paid invoices_   Media: _paper_

Personally Identifiable Information: ☐ Yes   ☒ No

Business Confidential: ☐ Yes   ☒ No

Original: ☒ Yes   ☐ No   Condition: _good_

Container Enclosure Type: _metal file cabinets_

Housing: _4-drawer lateral_   Type: _____

Specialty: ☐ Yes   ☒ No   Condition: _good_

Existing Dispersal: ☒ Yes   ☐ No

Where: _duplicate at Corporate Finance_

Problems Noted: _____

Record (2): _Customer billing_   Media: _electronic database_

Personally Identifiable Information: ☒ Yes   ☐ No

Business Confidential: ☐ Yes   ☒ No

Original: ☒ Yes   ☐ No   Condition: _good_

Container Enclosure Type: _LAN server_

Housing: _____   Type: _____

Specialty: ☐ Yes   ☒ No   Condition: _____

Existing Dispersal: ☒ Yes   ☐ No

Where: _back-up tape in media storage_

Problems Noted: _____

Electronic Equipment:

Type: _PC_   Info Media: _hard disk_

Use: _word processing, spreadsheets, database entry_

Brand/Model: _Banana 3000, Pentium 133_

Vendor: _Banana PCS Inc._   Serial #: _000123_

Standalone: ☐ Yes   ☒ No   Operating System: _Windows 400_

Info Backup: ☒ Yes   ☐ No

Back-up Method: _tape backup through LAN_

Location: _Backup Storage Inc._

Problems Noted: _____

Remarks:

_____

Figure 3.3b Site Survey (Page 2)

negotiating a contract for software site licenses, organizations need to allow for disaster recovery to ensure that software can be used at back-up sites or employees' homes.[13]

QUICK TIPS

• Reasonably priced computer software is available for PCs that detect and "clean" viruses from a system.

• PC files can be copied to a diskette, a flash drive, an external hard drive, or tape cartridges for backup. Portable tape cartridge drives can be purchased anywhere that computers are sold.

• Make sure that a copy of a back-up/ restore program is available for installation into any PC that will hold data restored from backups to the hard drive.

Large computing systems, such as mainframes and local and wide area networks, can be protected by magnetic tape back-up systems, electronic vaulting, and offsite storage. Electronic vaulting provides for the online, real-time duplication and transfer of critical data to a remote server or tape drive. Critical data can be transferred to a remote site on a real-time basis.[14]

Workstations, laptops, and hand-held computing devices can use the operating software's back-up utilities; special back-up software; or automatic, online back-up software. Good virus protection software and services are available to help prevent virus attacks, detect the presence of virus infections, and, in the event of a successful attack, aid in correcting the damage caused by a virus.

The easiest way to assess the strength of existing physical and environmental security and controls is to develop and conduct simulations. Base the simulations on the information researched for the risk analysis and risk assessment processes. The simulations help determine whether the mitigation and protection processes work the way they should and help identify any gaps in the protection of vital records and information.

Risk Analysis

Risk analysis identifies the *probabilities* of risk of damage to or loss of records and information. The risk analysis process involves:

- Identifying probable threats to records and information and analyzing the related vulnerabilities of records and information to these threats;

- Identifying the vulnerability of the organization to natural and other community-wide disasters (locality risks);

- Identifying the vulnerability of the organization to emergencies caused by acts of deliberate destructiveness, building or equipment failure or malfunction, and human error or carelessness.[15]

Analysis of potential disruptive events can help determine the potential liability the organization might be subject to, the likelihood that events will occur, and the consequences to the organization if they do occur. As a risk may have multiple causes, the parallels between each *risk* and its *cause* must be established. Subsequently, identifying and handling each risk with an identified cause as a separate risk event is often helpful.

Document identified risks on a formalized log, generally referred to as a *risk register*. A **risk register** is a table used to document risk information associated with an ongoing project. Generally constructed as a word processing document, sample field headings include *Risk Event, Date, Root Cause,* and *Probability.* Although content requirements for register entries vary from organization to organization, some consistency exists. Common among register entries are:

- The assigned code for each identified risk

- The risk category

- The risk identification date

- A risk description

- Assessment data

Natural disasters are the most unpredictable emergencies and require alternative information resources for protection. The type of organization also may imply potential risks. For example, fireworks manufacturing or volatile chemical manufacturing carry the risk of explosion and fire. Defense weapons development organizations can be the victims of sabotage or terrorism. A portion of a risk analysis is presented in Figure 3.4.

Facility	Risks	Probable Threats
Plant 1	• Fire • Water damage • Flood • Radiation leak • Tornado/Hurricane damage • Wrong chemical mixture during treatment process	• Hurricane • Tornado • Floods • Nuclear power plant within 10-mile radius • Treatment control system failure

Figure 3.4 A Portion of a Risk Analysis

Business Impact Analysis

The business impact analysis process involves identifying critical business functions and their supporting records and information and determining maximum acceptable loss beyond which the negative impact would be too great.

The analysis includes identifying potential threats to records and information and determining the probability of the occurrence of each threat through quantitative and qualitative analysis. The impact of the occurrence on each functional area can be rated using a scoring system that represents a comprehensive assessment of the risk. The most common score or rating is a combination of "high," "medium," and "low" impact and probability in a nine-cell matrix. A numeric rating is assigned to each of the nine cells in the matrix, giving a means of measuring the results of the analysis. General recommended actions for records and information can be assigned to each score. Estimated costs for each action can also be calculated, establishing a base for determining a cost analysis for proposed mitigation of records and information loss or vulnerability.

Figure 3.5 shows a nine-cell records and information impact and probability matrix that includes recommended actions for records and information for each score.

		Probability of Loss or Damage		
	Low	Low	Medium	High
Impact		**1** (Accept and monitor risk)	**2** (Protect **useful** and **important** records through management procedures)	**3** (Protect **useful** and **important** records through management procedures)
of **Loss** **or**	Medium	**4** (Recovery procedures for **important** records included in business continuity plan)	**5** (Reduce risk where possible; recovery procedures for **important** records included in business continuity plan)	**6** (Reduce risk; recovery procedures for **important** records included in business continuity plan)
Damage	High	**7** (Protect **vital** records; recovery procedures included in business continuity plan)	**8** (Reduce risk where possible; protect **vital** records; recovery procedures included in business continuity plan)	**9** (Reduce risk; protect **vital** records; recovery procedures included in business continuity plan)

Figure 3.5 Records and Information Impact and Probability Matrix

Figure 3.6 shows a sample impact/probability rating for each of the potential risks identified in the risk assessment.

Facility	Risks/Vulnerabilities	Impact/Probability Score
Plant 1	Fire • Old building – does not meet current codes • No equipment safety program	9
	Floods • Water damage • Building on flood plain of XYZ River	9
	Hurricane • Water damage • Structural damage	9
	Tornado • Structural damage	5
	Digital security • Old building – does not meet current codes	5
	Electronic data loss • Old building – does not meet current codes • No equipment safety program • Increased equipment downtime over past year	9
	Personal injury • No equipment safety program • Old building – does not meet current codes	9
	Equipment malfunction • No equipment safety program • Increased equipment downtime over past year	6
	Radiation leak • Nuclear power plant within 10-mile radius	6
	Earthquake • Structural damage	4
	Mudslide • Structural damage	2
	Tsunami • Water damage • Structural damage	2

Figure 3.6 Sample Impact/Probability Rating

Scoring results can be applied to the cost to protect the information assets from loss due to the occurrence of the most likely potential threats rated as having a high impact on each prioritized business process. The organization must set the minimum levels of records and information functionality it is willing to accept following a disruptive event based on its risk tolerance.

Evaluating the cost of loss of records and information involves appraising the financial value of several factors. The loss of vital records and information cost factors can include the following:

- Reconstruction or salvage time and expense
- Revenue losses and the loss of interest on the revenue
- Lost contracts and their monetary value
- Unproductive time
- Uncollectible accounts receivable
- Cost to respond to a personal information security breach
- Fines or restrictive measures for noncompliance with laws or regulations

DISASTER SNAPSHOT

A warehouse in an industrial complex housing six businesses near downtown Albuquerque, New Mexico, burned for several days after catching fire from a faulty heating/ventilation/cooling unit on the south side of the complex. The fire was so intense that the fire suppression system inside the 50-year-old building wasn't strong enough to put out the flames. The warehouse had six occupants: Cross Country Auto Parts, TMM Records Storage, Factory Motor Parts, a vacant business, and a warehouse. The fire destroyed one of the businesses—the TMM Business Records Storage and Management facility that stored more than 150,000 boxes of business documents. Two businesses were damaged—the records warehouse and Cross Country Auto Parts.

The University of New Mexico Hospital lost more than 100,000 medical records in the fire, and about 90 percent of the hospital's medical records dated before 2005. The fire burned for several days, and an estimated 40 percent of the records were destroyed at that time. A week later, the fire flared up again, and flames and more water destroyed everything else. Fortunately, the hospital switched to a digital system five years previously, and all records from 2005 to the present are electronically filed. Along with patient records, medical research documents were stored inside the warehouse. Hospital officials said that they don't know how many projects were lost, but they believe that the main researchers of the projects should have most of the data stored on computers.

Sources: KOAT TV, "National Team To Help Investigate Fire Documents Still Smoldering From Wednesday's Warehouse Fire," Albuquerque, NM (Posted: 4:02 PM MDT June 25, 2010; Updated: 5:45 PM MDT June 25, 2010). 4 March 2011 *<http://www.koat.com/r/24046306/detail.html>*; David Romero, KRQE TV. "Cause of 3-alarm warehouse fire unknown," Albuquerque, NM (Published: Wednesday, 23 Jun 2010, 8:47 PM MDT; Updated Thursday 24 Jun 2010, 6:34 PM MDT). 4 March 2011 *<http://www.krqe.com/dpp/news/crime/two-alarm-fire-rakes-downtown-warehouse>*; Kayla Anderson, KOB TV. "Feds called in to help investigate downtown fire," Albuquerque, NM (Posted at: 06/25/2010 6:52 PM). 3 March 2011 *<http://www.kob.com/article/stories/S1625640.shtml?cat=504>*.

In an effort to assess the impact of Hurricane Katrina on recordkeeping facilities, a tour of the Gulf Coast area of Mississippi was undertaken by representatives of the Council of State Archivists (CoSA), the Society of American Archivists (SAA), and Heritage Preservation. According to David Carmichael in "Lessons that Katrina Taught Me," at Pass Christian, Mississippi, "historians carefully placed the town's most historic records – maps, early photographs, Civil War records – in a bank vault as Hurricane Katrina approached. When the storm passed, the vault appeared to be intact, but its contents were ruined. The vault had been unable to withstand the water that surged through the building."

Lesson Learned

"Vaults that appear safe may not protect critical records."[16]

CHAPTER 3 CHECKLIST

Risk Analysis

☐ Identify probable threats to the organization and vital records information.

☐ Analyze related vulnerabilities of records and information to these threats.

☐ Identify the vulnerability of the organization to natural and other community-wide disasters.

☐ Identify the vulnerability of the organization to emergencies caused by acts of deliberate destructiveness, building or equipment failure or malfunction, and human error or carelessness.

Risk Assessment

☐ Evaluate existing physical and environmental security and controls.

☐ Assess the adequacy of existing security and controls relative to potential threats to records and information.

☐ Conduct a physical site survey to determine where security and controls exist and where potential hazards to records and information exist.

☐ Identify and recommend security and controls to protect records and information.

☐ Establish security and controls to protect vital records and information.

Business Impact Analysis

☐ Identify critical business functions.

☐ Determine the impact of the unavailability of records and information beyond the maximum acceptable outage.

☐ Determine the impact and probability scores.

☐ Determine costs to mitigate the loss of records and information for prioritized critical business processes.

NOTES

1. Victoria L. Lemieux, *Managing Risk for Records and Information* (Prairie Village: ARMA International, 2004), 1.

2. Dictionary.com, *Dictionary.com Unabridged.* Random House, Inc. 15 March 2011 *<http://dictionary.reference.com/browse/risk >*.

3. Lemieux, *Managing Risk for Records and Information*, 86.

4. Dennis I. Dickstein and Robert H. Flast, *No Excuses: A Business Process Approach to Managing Operational Risk* (New Jersey: Wiley, 2009), 81.

5. *Disaster Recovery Journal – Glossary.* 26 March 2011 *<http://www.drj.com/tools/tools/glossary-2.html>*.

6. *Disaster Recovery Journal – Glossary*, 13.

7. Michel Crouhy, Dan Galai, and Robert Market, *Risk Management* (New York: McGraw-Hill, 2001), 99.

8. Lemieux, *Managing Risk for Records and Information*, 35.

9. Geoffrey H. Wold and Robert F Shriver, "Risk Analysis Techniques," *Disaster Recovery Journal* 7, no. 3 (July/August/September 1994): 46.

10. Lemieux, *Managing Risk for Records and Information,* 64.

11. Factory Mutual Engineering & Research, "Taking Steps to Decrease the Risk of Office Fire Losses," *Disaster Recovery Journal* 5, no. 2 (April/May/June 1992): 9.

12. Dennis S. Deutsch, "Simple Yet Savvy," *Computerworld* 28, no. 40 (October 3, 1994): 121.

13. Mary F. Robek, Gerald F. Brown, and David O. Stephens, *Information and Records Management: Document-Based Systems,* 4th ed. (New York: Glencoe/McGraw–Hill, Inc., 1995), 85.

14. Robek, Brown, and Stephens, *Information and Records Management,* 82-83.

15. Robek, Brown, and Stephens, *Information and Records Management,* 46.

16. David W. Carmichael, "Lessons that Katrina Taught Me," Item 3, Meeting with Georgia municipal and court associations (November 2005).

Vital Records Program

"Whatever the media your vital records are on, and wherever they are stored, you must have a plan for safeguarding them and recovering them in the event of a disaster."[1]

Clearly, protecting all records and information in an organization would be difficult. Determining critical business processes and completing risk management processes are the first steps in developing a program to protect and recover critical records and information. A records and information disaster results in the loss of records and information essential to the organization's continued operation. Consequently, an emergency management or business continuity plan for records and information must include clearly identified vital records to best allocate resources for their protection and recovery.

Vital records are "records that are fundamental to the functioning of an organization. Certain vital records contain information critical to the continuation or survival of an organization during or immediately following a crisis. Such records are necessary to continue operations without delay under abnormal conditions. They contain information necessary to recreate an organization's legal and financial status and to preserve the rights and obligations of stakeholders, including employees, customers, investors, and citizens…The term *vital records* also includes documentation subject to a vital records program, such as pertinent IT systems, help manuals, or emergency contact lists. For the purposes of this standard, the use of this term does *not* mean solely those birth and death records referred to as "vital records" in the vital statistics or health industry."[2]

As discussed in Section I, critical business processes and their supporting records and information must be safeguarded. Once the critical business processes of an organization are understood, the vital records are easier to identify. Many people, however, tend to overestimate the value of organizational information. Approximately 5 to 10 percent of the records created by an organization are considered vital and are necessary to resume business.[3] Other records may be important, but they are not vital.

Accurate identification of vital information is critical because this information:

- Establishes the legal status of the organization as a business entity.
- Documents the assets and liabilities of the organization from a financial perspective.
- Documents the operations of the organization, which enable production processes or other work to be accomplished.[4]

An effective vital records management program includes:

- Descriptions of all vital records necessary to protect assets and ensure continuity of business operations.
- Documentation of procedures and practices followed to protect and restore these records.
- Adequate operating instructions to permit the effective use of selected records in an emergency.[5]

Vital Records Management Program Development

A vital records management program can be developed during emergency or business continuity planning, or it can be approached as a separate project. Some organizations initiate vital records management programs because they are required by law or regulation. For example, most financial institutions are required by law to have a plan or program to protect critical records, and federal agencies are required by regulation to establish vital records management programs. Regardless of when the program is established, it should be incorporated as part of the overall organizational emergency management or business continuity plan.

ARMA International has established guidelines for developing and implementing vital records management programs, and the process is also described in detail in several records management textbooks. The selected bibliography in Appendix C includes additional publications that can assist in understanding vital records management program planning. This chapter presents only those aspects of vital records management programs that are important to emergency management and business continuity planning.

The process of developing a vital records management program includes:

- Assigning program responsibilities

- Completing risk management processes

- Identifying and compiling a list of vital records

- Selecting protection methods and remote storage locations and developing strategies to ensure protection of the vital records

- Preparing a vital records matrix

- Developing procedures and practices to be followed to protect these records and to permit effective use of selected records in an emergency

- Documenting vital records management program policy and procedures

Assign Program Responsibilities

The vital records program responsibilities should be assigned to the person who is authorized to perform vital records program tasks relative to the entire organization. The records and information manager (position title varies with each organization) is the logical project leader for establishing a vital records management program. In some organizations, this person performs all tasks necessary to produce the vital records management program and the records and information elements of the emergency management or business continuity plan. Smaller organizations may include vital records management program planning in the project scope of an emergency management or business continuity planning team or as a task assignment for an individual.

In large organizations, the records and information manager may work in conjunction with a records management team or committee whose primary responsibility is the establishment of a comprehensive records management program. Vital records management and records and information emergency management or business continuity are usually parts of the comprehensive program.

The records and information manager is responsible for developing, implementing, maintaining, and updating the vital records management program. The manager must work closely with each section of the organization to implement and maintain vital records protection and emergency management or business continuity procedures. He or she should also be prepared to liaise with emergency services

QUICK TIPS

- Assign one person who can function as records manager for vital records purposes. For example, an administrative assistant, the office manager, or the administrative services manager may serve in a dual role as records manager as well.

- Use the direct approach of classifying vital records into either vital or nonvital categories (method 2).

- Back up all PCs at least weekly and store back-up disks or tape cartridges in an offsite location such as a bank vault or another organization-owned location.

- Place small volumes of vital records into a fire-resistant cabinet or safe each night to provide some protection against loss.

to apprise them of the location of the vital records and the procedures for accessing and recovering them. If the organization fails following a disaster, the records and information manager is often required to help locate information or explain records management policy and procedures in legal or audit situations.

Complete Risk Management Processes

The cost of protecting or reconstructing vital records must be weighed against the value of the information to the organization. The risk management processes discussed in Chapter 3 are essential for determining the vulnerabilities of vital records and information. They are important for establishing adequate protection and for deciding the value of records and information.

Identify Vital Records

Vital records management programs play an important part in the life cycle of records because the value of information may change as the data ages. A vital records management program, therefore, is more effective when built on an implemented records retention schedule and records disposition plan. Vital records are not necessarily permanent records. They are necessary for the continuation of business processes following a disruptive event, and, therefore, should be the most current records and data. Many vital records are active, short-term retention records.

Identification of essential records requires agreement among executives as to which information is vital to the organization. Records and information that support critical business processes are logically included in a vital records program. The records showing testing results of water quality, for example, would support water treatment processes considered critical for a water utility, and would therefore be considered vital records for that organization.

Although legally valuable records must be protected, most records are considered vital only during the most active stage. Records should be classified as vital only for as long as they support critical business processes and fulfill the requirements described in the definition. Once they have fulfilled this role, they should be reclassified.[6] Restoration of obsolete or out-of-date records and information will not help an organization effectively recover from a disruptive event. Activity and vital priorities decrease the longer a record is kept. Following records disposition procedures to purge obsolete records and information makes identifying, isolating, and protecting current vital records easier.

Some examples of vital records and information commonly found in most organizations include:

- Current accounts receivable and accounts payable records
- Ownership records for land, facilities, equipment, and vehicles
- Current contracts and agreements
- Current personnel and payroll records
- Current customer or client records
- Tax records
- Unaudited accounting transactions
- Standard operating procedures or directives

> Remember—vital records management program documentation and emergency management and business continuity plans are always considered vital records!

Select Protection Methods and Remote Storage

Different types of records and information media provide challenges to emergency or business continuity planning efforts. Distinctive conditions for protecting the information contained on each media type require special attention. Magnetic media and microfilm must be stored in closely controlled environments to prevent damage over time. Electronic records are affected by power outages, unauthorized intrusion, electrical surges or drains, and static electricity. Therefore, they require other forms of protection.

Safeguarding information on existing media may not be feasible, and alternative media may need to be selected. Paper is subject to as much environmentally-caused damage as other media, but the volume of paper records makes controlled or duplicate storage costly. Microfilming or electronically imaging vital paper records, for instance, can reduce controlled storage and security duplication costs.

Early generations of hardware and application software incompatible with current generations of hardware and application software may make recovery of electronic media difficult. Locating older computer systems for information restoration following a disruptive event may not be possible, resulting in irretrievable data. Additionally, data created with older or obsolete software may not be recoverable if the software is lost or destroyed. Migrating long-term retention data to new software applications, as they are implemented, aids in timely recovery of the information.

Because each vital record must be protected using a specified method, the best way to protect vital information is by remote storage of back-up data or records. Some records and data may already have an existing method of backup or duplication and distribution. When existing duplication or protection is not available, the most cost-effective methods of duplication/protection for vital records and information must be determined. Wherever possible, incorporate existing methods of backup, duplication, and protection into the vital records management program.

DISASTER SNAPSHOT

Companies touting online medical records to consumers are using hurricane Katrina as a selling point: A disaster, they say, can destroy medical records kept in doctors' offices or make them otherwise unavailable. "It's a solution that works today that would have addressed every single issue that came out of (the) recent disasters of Katrina and Rita," says Robert Lorsch, a Los Angeles businessman and founder of *MyMedicalRecords.com*.

With Internet-based records, Lorsch says, evacuees would have been able to trace their medical histories and pull up their prescriptions as soon as they were able to connect to the Web.

Source: Julie Appleby, "Don't let hurricanes blow your medical records away, companies say," USAToday, Money Section, 27 October 2005, 3B.

Vital records protection usually involves one of three methods: (1) dispersal, (2) protective storage, or (3) electronic protective storage. **Dispersal** is the routine or designed transfer of duplicate records to locations other than those where the originals are housed.[7] **Routine dispersal** is dispersal of duplicate records as part of normal business practice such as recording land conveyance records at a county courthouse. Using routine dispersal as protection adds little or no additional cost to the organization. However, routinely dispersed duplicates must be kept current and accessible. **Designed dispersal** is a duplicate records dispersal procedure established specifically to protect vital information such as sending microfilm duplicates to a branch office for storage or the scheduled creation of back-up tapes for electronic files. Cost of designed dispersal is determined by the media to be duplicated, the volume of records and information, and the availability and cost of the dispersal location.

Protective storage involves the use of fire-resistant and environmentally-controlled records protection equipment and vaults designed for the protection of the media being stored. **Records protective equipment** are self-contained, movable devices of varying configurations, including insulated bodies with insulated doors or drawers or lids, nonrated multidrawer devices housing individually-rated bodies, and other similar constructions.[8] The storage can be either onsite or offsite. Onsite protective storage allows active vital records to be maintained near the users, without costly planned dispersal. However, the storage may be subject to denial of access by local authorities or emergency services following an event, depending on the nature of the disruptive event.

Offsite storage of hard media records usually involves contracting with a storage provider or constructing an organization-owned facility in another location. Offsite storage facilities must meet all fire and collapsing structure protective requirements. Some organizations share the cost of constructing and maintaining vital records facilities with other organizations with similar vital information protection needs. Protection of vital records requires the records to be duplicated and stored in offsite storage so that if the originating location is damaged or destroyed, the only copy of the information is not lost. Offsite protective storage is more effective if the media is stored in appropriate environmental conditions that meet American National Standards Institute (ANSI) or

International Organization for Standardization (ISO) standards and the location is readily accessible, including after business hours.

In the U.S., adequate fire-resistive file housing and vaults used for protective storage must meet the rating requirements of the National Fire Protection Association (NFPA). The NFPA requires records protection equipment to be moveable and includes fire-resistant safes and cabinets. The equipment must be listed or labeled as "protection equipment" in accordance with the standard.

The equipment is classified in terms of an interior temperature limit and the time in hours before combustion of the contents. For example, a Class 125, two-hour vault will protect the contents for two hours at 125°F. The appropriate classification equipment must be used for the media it contains. NFPA-252 notes, for example, that magnetic media should be stored in Class 150 equipment.[9]

NFPA-232 requires vital records to be stored in either fire-resistant equipment or standard records vaults. **Standard records vaults** are completely fire-resistive enclosures used exclusively for records storage. Standard records vaults must be equipped, maintained, and supervised to minimize the possibility of origin of fire within and to prevent entrance of fire from outside for a specified period of time. The vault must be constructed according to specified ratings.[10] Care must be taken to purchase fire-resistive housing or construct vaults that meet these requirements, or records may not be adequately protected.

Electronic protective storage involves transmitting original electronic data and/or files not contained on tape, optical disk, or other magnetic or optical physical media, to offsite electronic storage. Electronic protective storage methods include electronic vaulting and data replication.

Electronic vaulting is the transfer of data to an alternative server for storage in a data warehouse or electronic vault. A **data warehouse** is a central repository for all or selected data created, used and often maintained by the organization. The warehouse can either be on a separate server within the organization's domain or on a commercial provider owned server accessed through telecommunications. Most commercial providers of electronic vaulting offer the service through the Internet or other electronic transfer using encryption and security codes. Once the data is received, an authorized user must decrypt the data. **Encryption** is the conversion of data into cipher text meeting national and international standards that cannot be easily understood by unauthorized users or viewers. **Decryption** is the process of converting encrypted data back into its original form using a predetermined decryption key based on an algorithm.

Data replication is the process of replicating data between two or more sites to be used in the event the primary site is unavailable. The most common methods of replication are transaction-aware replication, mirroring, and shadowing. **Transaction-aware replication** electronically transmits database or file changes to the secondary site and applies the changes to a replicated dataset. **Mirroring** maintains an exact copy of electronic records by applying changes to the database or files at a secondary site synchronous to changes at the primary site. This method requires more bandwidth to process the data than shadowing. **Shadowing** maintains an exact copy of electronic records by continuously capturing changes to the database or files and applying them to the secondary site.[11] Shadowing is an asynchronous method (i.e., transmitted intermittently rather than in steady stream) and requires less bandwidth than mirroring.

Alan A. Andolsen, CMC, CRM, in an *Information Management Journal* article, recommends concentrating on four important principles in the protection of digital records:

1. All vital digital records must be clearly identified by the information owner and the information system operator and appropriate protection responsibilities assigned.

2. Periodic audits of the protection process must be scheduled to assure that the digital records are being protected as specified in the procedures.

3. Correct maintenance procedures must be in place to ensure that the digital information is not compromised by inappropriate environmental storage conditions.

4. Appropriate equipment must be selected for housing, transporting, and storing vital digital records.[12]

Prepare Vital Records Matrix

Once the critical records and information are identified, information about them must be compiled into a form that can be used to apply protection methods and to speed recovery after a disruptive event. A **vital records matrix** is a detailed list identifying vital documents, their location, protection instructions, method of protection, classification and priority, and recovery responsibility in case the records are lost during a disruptive event. A portion of a vital records matrix is shown in Figure 4.1.

The schedule should adequately provide enough information about each vital record type to assist in protection of the record and planning and implementing response and recovery procedures. Some organizations will place a response and recovery priority on highly referenced records, and records containing personal or confidential information must be handled appropriately during response and recovery.

Preparation of a vital records matrix requires several steps: inventory, analyze, classify, set priorities, select media, select protection method, and compile the schedule. A vital records inventory may be part of a complete records inventory, or it may be a separate process. Establishing a vital records management program is much easier to do when records series and retentions are already in place, and records and information supporting critical business processes have been identified.

A *vital records inventory* contains data useful for determining vital information and the degree to which the information is protected. A vital records inventory includes:

- A list of all records and information, their purpose, and description; for example:

    Paid Invoices—original paper records showing to whom billed, date of billing, services/ products provided, date shipped, amount of invoice, date paid, and amount paid. Used for collection of accounts receivable, audit, and legal purposes.

- The business process they support.

- Reference activity and frequency.

- The location of the records and information, designating originals and duplicates, and the type of media.

- Information or documentation necessary to reconstruct and/or access the vital record.

- Identification of records containing personally identifiable, confidential, or sensitive information.

- Software and version required to access electronic vital records; type of protection required.

- The existing duplication and/or dispersal and existing protection and assessed vulnerabilities.

- Anticipated annual cost of maintaining protection for the records and information.

As data collected for the vital records inventory are analyzed, the records are classified, and vital records and information are identified. Records critical to immediate functioning of the organization can be determined by reviewing the records and information that support identified critical business processes. For example, a law firm may determine that current court docket schedules, cases in progress, and billing data may be necessary to resume business immediately following a disruptive event. Examples of records that may be critical to specific types of organizations are listed in Figure 4.2.

The process of identifying and classifying vital records includes:

- Determining the records and information essential to the immediate resumption of business following a disruptive event.

- Determining the records and information essential for legal or fiscal purposes and records that support critical business processes.

- Classifying vital records according to the degree of importance to immediate resumption of business, as well as the importance of the business process they support.

- Determining any existing methods of duplication/protection.

- Determining the most cost-effective methods of duplication/protection for identified vital records.

Record Identifier	Record	Location	Media	Electronic Application	Reference Activity	Personal or Confidential Information	Protection	Classification and Priority	Recovery Responsibility
V1000	Daily customer transactions	Customer service	Digital/ e-server	PUBS 2	High	No	Nightly backup to XYZ data vault via secured modem (www.xyz.com)	Class 1 Vital A	IT obtains from contingency storage and restores data onto e-server
V1001	Legal cases, originals	Central records	Paper	N/A	High	Yes	Microfilm original stored at ABC Records Storage	Class 1 Vital A	RM obtains originals from contingency storage, creates duplicates; central files supervisor places duplicates into files
V1002	Paid invoices, originals	Accounts receivable	Paper	N/A	Medium	No	Duplicate on file in Corporate Finance – New York	Class 1 Vital B	RM obtains copies of duplicates from corporate; accounting supervisor places duplicates into files
V1003	Billing files, originals	Accounts receivable	LAN "I" drive	MS Excel 2003	High	Yes	Nightly tape backup of LAN, stored at Backup Storage Inc.	Class 1 Vital A	RM obtains from contingency storage; network admin. restores files to network
V1004	Deeds to land, owner copies	File vault	Paper	N/A	Medium	No	Original on file in county courthouse	Class 1 Vital B	RM obtains duplicates from courthouse originals and places into vault

Figure 4.1 Sample Vital Records Matrix

Organization Type	Record
Law Firm	Current client case files Original legal research documentation Current court dockets Briefs in progress Billing records
Medical Center	Patient files Laboratory tests in progress Insurance and billing records
Water Utility	Water treatment data Water quality monitoring data Water distribution system data

Figure 4.2 Organization-Specific Vital Records Examples

The process of classifying vital records includes establishing a continuum of vital, important, useful, and nonessential records. A sample records classification is shown in Figure 4.3. Vital records are fundamental to the function of an organization. **Important records** assist in performing an organization's business operations and, if destroyed, may be replaced at considerable cost. **Useful records** are helpful in conducting business operations and, if destroyed, may be replaced at slight cost. **Nonessential records** on a variety of media are considered to be of little value to an organization. These records are usually for convenience only and not vital to the operations or existence of the organization. Examples include routine telephone messages, employee bulletins, reading files, and various announcements.

Class	Definition	Example	Example Protection Method
CLASS 1: Vital	• Records contain information essential to the continuation or survival of an organization during or immediately following a crisis. • Such records are necessary to continue operations without delay under abnormal conditions. • They contain information necessary to recreate an organization's legal and financial status and to preserve the rights and obligations of stakeholders, including employees, customers, investors, and citizens. • Vital status should be assigned only for as long as they fulfill the above requirements. Once they have fulfilled this role, they should be reclassified.	• Current accounts payable and accounts receivable • Current customer or client files • Research documentation • Current contracts and agreements • Unaudited financial records	• Back-up tape stored offsite • Back-up tape and back-up microfilm stored offsite • Back-up files from imaging server sent by electronic transmission to a remote electronic vault • Ledgers and transaction documentation stored in a standard record vault • Original records transferred to offsite protective storage and surrogate copies used for reference
CLASS 2: Important	• Records necessary to the continued life of the business. • They can be replaced or reproduced only at considerable cost in time and money.	• Ownership records for land, facilities, equipment, and vehicles • Tax records	• Backup of imaging media stored offsite • Routine and planned dispersal
CLASS 3: Useful	• Records useful to the uninterrupted operation of the business. • They are replaceable, but their loss could cause temporary inconvenience.	• Bank statements • Correspondence	• Routine dispersal

Figure 4.3 Sample Records Classification[13]

For many organizations, the speed of response to a disruptive event relies on quick access to vital records. The extent to which emergency planning and recovery procedures are applied to vital records depends on organizational need. Deciding the appropriate applications relies on accurate assignment of priorities to all identified vital records and information. Records classified as vital can be allocated one of three priorities—A, B, or C—as shown in Figure 4.4. Nonvital records are not assigned a class and are not included on the vital records matrix.

Vital Records Priorities			
Priority	**Definition**	**Access**	**Example**
Vital A	• Records and information essential for emergency operations	• Physical protective storage close to disaster response site for very quick access • Electronic replication methods available for immediate access of information	• Emergency action plan, business continuity plan, vital records manual • Current facility drawings • Personnel security clearance lists • Emergency management communication lists and personnel contact lists • Customer contact information • Community and regional maps
Vital B	• Records and information essential for immediate resumption and continuation of business following a disaster	• Physical protective storage close to the disaster recovery site for quick business resumption • Electronic replication methods quickly accessible • Backups quickly restored	• Current customer or client files • In-progress accounts payable and accounts receivable • Research documentation • Current contracts and agreements
Vital C	• Records and information essential for legal or audit purposes	• Physical protective storage accessible and outside the disaster area	• Accounts payable and accounts receivable files • Existing contracts and agreements • Unaudited financial records

Figure 4.4 Sample Vital Records Priorities

Emergency operation records include selected records and information necessary to continue the most critical business functions and related policy or procedural records. These records assist the organization in operating under emergency conditions and in resuming normal operation after the emergency.

As discussed in Section I, recovery procedures include two phases. Recovery phase one procedures are necessary for short-term, immediate response. Vital records, class 1 (V1 records) are used during this phase. In most cases, these records and information must be retrieved from temporary, emergency storage and distributed to temporary operation centers. Recovery phase two procedures include the retrieval or recovery of V2 and V3 records.

Establish Procedures

A vital records management program is only effective when it is used. Specific procedures must be established for each step in the process of developing and maintaining the vital records management program. The vital records matrix and specific procedures for the retrieval of backups and the restoration of information after a disruptive event has occurred should be included in the records and information emergency management or business continuity plan. A typical vital records and disaster recovery flow model is shown in Figure 4.5. The remaining chapters of this book discuss the preparation, response, and recovery phases for emergency management and business continuity.

Vital Records and Disaster Recovery Flow Model

1. Vital Records Program *(Prevention)*
   - Assign program responsibilities
   - Complete risk management processes
   - Identify and compile list of vital records
   - Select protection strategies and methods
   - Prepare a vital records matrix
     — Classify
     — Set priorities
   - Develop protection procedures
   - Develop procedures for use of vital records in an emergency
   - Document vital records policy and procedures
     — Vital records manual
   - Develop loss prevention plan
     — Determine
       ○ Alternative location
       ○ Alternative data source
       ○ Recovery and salvage service provider
       ○ Prepare & implement plan
       ○ Test & update plan

2. Emergency Management or Business Continuity Plan *(Preparation)*
   - Prepare and implement the plan
     — Incorporate records & information loss prevention plan
   - Update and test the plan

3. Activate the emergency management or business continuity plan when necessary. *(Response)*

4. Recovery Steps *(Recovery)*
   - Access damage
   - Stabilize
   - Salvage
   - Restore
   - Resume operations

Figure 4.5 Vital Records and Disaster Recovery Flow Model

Document Vital Records Management Program Policy and Procedures

Once these elements have been developed, they should be compiled into a vital records manual for easy reference. The vital records manual serves as a reference for all policies and procedures of the vital records program. At a minimum, the manual should include:[14]

- Names and positions of personnel assigned vital records responsibilities

- Completed risk management analyses

- Vital records matrix

- Established protection methods and strategies

- Specific procedures for the retrieval of dispersed copies

- Established procedures for use of vital records in an emergency

- Procedures for the recovery and restoration of records and information after the occurrence of a disastrous event

- Emergency contact list of key personnel and service/recovery contractors (including physical addresses, e-mail addresses, phone and pager numbers)

- Disaster recovery firm contingency contract (if one exists)

- Site or facility maps (indicating location of vital records)

- Copy of the loss prevention plan

The manual can be used for audit and periodic review of the program, for training personnel and for providing direction during and immediately following an emergency. A copy of the manual should be retained with collections of vital records and stored in an appropriately protected environment. A log indicating to whom the manuals are assigned should be maintained. Keep this log current and include the dates when revisions are distributed for insertion into the manual.

The vital records manual should be reviewed annually (at a minimum) and revised when necessary. If the vital records program is part of the business continuity plan, the manual should be reviewed and updated to reflect changes in the plan as they occur. The individual responsible for timely manual updates should be included in the distribution of pertinent new or revised data and information as it is released within the organization.

DISASTER SNAPSHOT

Following the January 2010 earthquake, funding from UNESCO enabled the Haitian National Archives to relocate some of the most endangered documents from its damaged Bicentenaire Building to boxes as a protective measure. The transfer of these documents enabled the Archives to recommence some of its vital work relating to the management of civil status and registry documents. The funds also permitted the Archives to receive governmental records from some of the Ministries and other public institutions that collapsed following the earthquake. The National Library also received funding for similar emergency activities involving libraries, which were destroyed or demolished as a safety precaution. Considerable quantities of important documents still under rubble were in danger of being permanently lost if not located and placed into watertight storage prior to the start of the rainy season.

Source: Joie Springer, "UNESCO provides assistance in preserving Haitian documentary heritage," UNESCO.ORG, 01-03-2010. 19 March 2011 <http://portal.unesco.org/ci/en/ev.php-URL_ID=29582&URL_DO=DO_topic&url_section=201.html>.

Hurricane Katrina caused significant damage to court records in Jackson County, Mississippi. As these vital records had not been backed up and stored in an offsite location, the only viable option was records recovery. The $2 million recovery cost was expensive and unnecessary.[15]

Lesson Learned
Prevention measures are less expensive than recovery efforts.

CHAPTER 4 CHECKLIST

☐ Understand the definition of a vital record.

☐ Identify critical business processes and vital records.

☐ Assign vital records management program responsibilities.

☐ Complete risk management processes.

☐ Complete a vital records inventory.

☐ Select protection methods.

☐ Select back-up storage location and procedures.

☐ Prepare a vital records matrix.

☐ Establish vital records procedures.

NOTES

1. Michael Wallace and Lawrence Webber, *The Disaster Recovery Handbook: A Step-by-step Plan to Ensure Business Continuity and Protect Vital Operations, Facilities and Assets* (New York: AMACOM, 2004), xi.

2. ARMA International, ANSI/ARMA 5-2010, *Vital Records: Identifying, Managing, and Recovering Business-Critical Records* (Overland Park: ARMA), 5.

3. Thomas F. Lee, "Master the Disaster!" *Office Systems95* 12, no. 4 (April 1995): 16.

4. Mary F. Robek, Gerald F. Brown, and David O. Stephens, *Information and Records Management: Document-Based Information Systems,* 4th ed. (New York: Glencoe/McGraw Hill, Inc., 1995), 69.

5. Richard E. Wolff, "Snap, Crackle & Pop," *ARMA Records Management Quarterly* 19, no. 2 (April 1985): 4.

6. ARMA International, *Vital Records,* 6.

7. ARMA International, *Vital Records,* 3.

8. ARMA International, *Vital Records,* 4.

9. National Fire Protection Association, Inc., NFPA 232, *Protection of Records* (Quincy: National Fire Protection Association, Inc., 2000), 232-13, 232-8-21.

10. National Fire Protection Association, Inc., *Protection of Records,* 232-11, 232-5, 232-8.

11. ARMA International, *Vital Records,* 3, 4.

12. Alan A. Andolsen, CMC, CRM, "The Pillars of Vital Records Protection," *The Information Management Journal* (March/April 2008), 32.

13. Andolsen, "Pillars of Vital Records Protection," 12.

14. ARMA International, *Vital Records,* 16-17.

15. David W. Carmichael, "Lessons that Katrina Taught Me," Item 7, Meeting with Georgia municipal and court associations (November 2005).

Loss Prevention Plan

"Prevention programs outline tasks and responsibilities necessary to support and maintain an effective ongoing contingency program before a localized disaster occurs."[1]

A **loss prevention plan** is a written, approved, implemented, and periodically tested program specifically outlining all actions to be taken to reduce the risk of avoidable disaster and to minimize the loss if a disruptive event occurs. The plan is an essential element of the mitigation phase of emergency management and business continuity planning and is based on vital records and risk management processes. It includes the vital records matrix; results of risk analysis, risk assessment, and business impact analysis; detailed protective measures; and loss prevention procedures.

A written loss prevention plan based on a vital records program and risk management processes forms the mitigation phase of an effective emergency management or business continuity program. It is an integral part of the records and information emergency management or business continuity plan. All identified probabilities, existing vulnerabilities, and resulting corrective or protection action must be addressed in the loss prevention plan. With a good loss prevention plan, recovery following a disruptive event can be minimal.

A loss prevention plan provides direction for reducing the risk to records and information from natural and human hazards. The purpose of the plan is to *prevent* the loss of vital records and information, to *prevent* costly salvage of vital records and information, to *prevent* the delay of restoring critical business processes following a disruptive event, and to *prevent* or significantly minimize loss due to identified vulnerabilities and hazards. The plan addresses the appropriate measures necessary to protect records and information and the appropriate actions necessary to respond to a disruptive event.

The same amount of time and effort should be devoted to planning to prevent a disaster as is devoted to responding to or recovering from a disruptive event. Loss prevention is as difficult to cost-justify as disaster recovery, although more immediate results from prevention measures sometimes can be shown. Installing a new fire suppression system, for instance, can both improve employee safety and improve records protection. Often, loss prevention planning can be combined with business process improvement, which benefits the organization as a whole.

A loss prevention plan for facilities, such as commercial records centers housing backups of records and information that are used for the resumption of business following a disaster, is essential. The plan should be tailored to the specific operation, and all employees should participate fully in the preparation and testing of the plan.

Some organizations contain loss prevention for records and information within a business resumption plan. **Business resumption planning** (BRP) is the process of planning and preparing with the

DISASTER SNAPSHOT

Planning for prevention of records and information loss depends upon forecasting potential threats and disruptive events. Often, prevention strategies for the potential impact of an event is based on the occurrence of one type of event (hurricane, flood, fire, earthquake, etc.), rather than multiple types. In March 2011, Japan experienced a major earthquake. The country is well known for its planning and prevention strategies for earthquakes and should have been able to respond and recover from the event very quickly. Unfortunately, the earthquake triggered a 32-foot tsunami wave in the north part of the country. This combination of quake and tsunami triggered events that resulted in catastrophic damage to nuclear reactors at several electric power plants, including severe damage to the Fukushima Daiichi electric power plant. Consequently, Japan not only had to deal with the growing nuclear event but also with the loss of 30 percent of its electric power generation.

The domino effect of the impact of the events resulted in technology infrastructure being damaged or reduced in capacity, making business recovery very difficult. In addition, many of the world's major high tech manufacturers located in Japan had to stop production to carry out safety checks and endure rolling blackouts causing further interruptions. Sony, Panasonic, Toshiba, and Canon were among the companies affected not only by the power loss but also, in some cases, by damage from the quake and tsunami. Panasonic Corporation reported that ongoing aftershocks prevented it from inspecting two factories in northern Japan.

Sony confirmed that it had voluntarily suspended operations at seven manufacturing plants while the country assessed the state of its power grid. The company's Sendai Technology Centre in Tagajo, Miyagi Prefecture (one of the hardest hit areas of the country) was also closed due to earthquake damage. Three of Canon's plants sustained serious damage in the earthquake. These plants make LCD screens, lenses, and inkjet printers.

Much of the fixed communications infrastructure survived remarkably intact. Internet services were largely unaffected by the disaster. The seas around Japan are a major hub for undersea telecom cables, forming a critical part of the global Internet. While the earthquake caused damage to several sub-sea cables, most of Japan's cable landing stations are well south of Tokyo, or on the other side of the sheltered inlet that becomes Tokyo Bay.

Other parts of Japan's communication infrastructure were damaged. Telephone operator NTT East Japan reported that 879,000 telephony lines went out of service, as well as 475,400 fibre-optic lines, and more than 11,000 wireless base stations belonging to DoCoMo, KDDI, and Softbank were still out of service several days after the events.

Source: BBC News, "Japan earthquake disrupts technology companies," United Kingdom (Published 14 March 2011; Last updated at 14:56 ET). 15 March 2011, *<http://www.bbc.co.uk/news/technology-12731320>*.

goal of minimizing loss in the event of a disaster. The organization's vital functions are identified, and measures are taken to ensure that functions can be quickly and effectively restored.

Effective business resumption planning focuses on business processes. A BRP identifies critical processes without which the organization cannot serve its customers. It identifies the business resources required to perform these processes effectively and efficiently and also establishes reasonable alternative sources of the critical resources.[2]

Effective BRP focuses on discovering:

• The business processes performed, with supporting records and information identified;

- Those critical processes without which the organization cannot serve its customers;

- The business resources required to perform these processes effectively and efficiently;

- The means by which the company can reduce its need for those resources; and

- Reasonable alternative sources of the critical resources.[3]

Develop a Loss Prevention Plan

For a loss prevention plan to be effective, it should contain certain basic components for maximum effectiveness. A loss prevention plan has five key components:

1. A clear policy statement

2. Procedures for mitigating and monitoring potential hazards and destructive forces

3. Procedures for monitoring relevancy of ongoing prevention, response, and recovery contracts

4. Provisions for training employees and testing the plans

5. Provisions for ongoing review and revision

A clear policy statement or directive from top management will signal approval of the plan and identify it as an official organizational policy. The policy should clearly mandate the preparation and implementation of the loss prevention plan. The mandate may be needed to secure the necessary resources and cooperation among departments, to have the authority to examine business processes and functions, to execute mitigation measures, to assign the organization resources needed for preparing an effective plan, and to authorize changes in organizational policies and procedures.

The loss prevention plan should be developed with the aid of the emergency management or business continuity planning team. Outside expertise from vendors and consultants may also be helpful. Responsibility for developing and implementing the loss prevention plan should be clearly defined in the policy statement. The responsibility may be given to the records manager, the records management team or committee, or the emergency management or business continuity team.

After the risk management procedures have been completed, the organization should take measures to correct or eliminate identified vulnerabilities and hazards. These measures should be regularly monitored to detect any changes since the last inspection. Procedures should be in place to monitor natural events, such as hurricanes, volcanic eruption, and flood warnings, so that appropriate preparedness steps can begin well in advance of the event. Appropriate security measures should be implemented and monitored to protect computer systems and data.

Ongoing prevention, response, and recovery contracts must be monitored for relevancy to the current needs of the organization. Ongoing prevention contracts can include vital records storage and insect/rodent monitoring and extermination contracts. Response and recovery contracts cover equipment, supplies, and services required by the emergency management or business continuity plan. Contracts for alternative operation or recovery sites should be monitored to assure adequate coverage meeting current electronic system needs. After each test of the emergency management or business continuity plan or actual event occurrence, vendor performance should be evaluated. Poor performers should be replaced or their contracts revised to cover the problem areas.

Employees should be trained as soon as the loss prevention plan is implemented. Employee training should include an understanding of loss prevention procedures, recognition of potential threats or existing vulnerabilities, and recognition of an impending emergency or disruptive event. Drills are essential to ensure quick and appropriate action within the organization.

Regular and frequent review and revision of the plan will help ensure that the plan, once activated, will be the tool it was intended to be. Maintaining a current list of names and telephone numbers of individuals and contractors as well as computer system needs is critical. Procedures must be kept current as business operations change.

Implement the Loss Prevention Plan

Implementation of a well-organized loss prevention plan will significantly reduce the cost of recovery and can avert or reduce the need for salvage following a disruptive event. Planned prevention averts the loss of vital records and information at the least possible cost. Therefore, loss prevention plans should be developed specifically for each organization.

All identified corrective and preventive measures should be put into place so that records and information are safeguarded and the response phase of the emergency management or business continuity plan can be activated when necessary.

The loss prevention plan also must establish the activities necessary to reduce or eliminate existing hazards to records and information within the bounds of the organization's risk tolerance. All vulnerabilities identified by the risk management process must be addressed, and corrective measures must be developed and achieved. Potential hazards to records and information must be eliminated wherever possible. Where hazards cannot be eliminated, records and information should either be moved to a safer location or duplicated, and electronic records should be secured with appropriate protection. In order to maintain a timely prevention program, the site survey should be updated at least once a year.

> **QUICK TIP**
>
> A small business owner may not have the resources available to undertake a comprehensive approach to the emergency management principles contained in the publication. However, any business owner can evaluate the priorities and determine which elements must be protected in order to remain in business if a disaster occurs.

Corrective measures take two directions. Some hazards to records and information are correctable—leaky roofs, lack of surge protectors, lack of fire suppression system, or insect intrusion. Some hazards are site-specific, and the records must be removed from the proximity of the hazard—water and sewer pipes, lack of heating or air-conditioning, building construction, use of nonstorage environment for records storage. Vital paper records can be protected using the dispersal or storage methods discussed in Chapter 4.

Electronic media and microforms can be easily damaged if improperly handled or stored. Both microfilm and electronic media have specific environmental requirements to prevent damage or loss. To protect vital records on electronic media or microfilm, first determine the environmental conditions necessary to protect each medium; then decide the optimum conditions to meet the requirements of all media. Choose a storage environment that meets the optimum conditions.

Choosing the appropriate protection method for electronic records is a critical step. Although most organizations would prefer to implement complete data replication alternatives to protect electronic records and information, the cost to do so is not always feasible.

Other loss prevention activities can be implemented to reduce vulnerabilities. These activities include:

- Employee training to prevent human error, unsafe work procedures, or carelessness
- Frequent building and equipment inspections and proper maintenance to avoid building and equipment malfunctions
- Implementation of building security measures to reduce adverse consequences during a natural disaster
- Implementation of an information security program to protect information from theft or vandalism
- Implementation of data and security breach response procedures for personal information
- Letting prevention, recovery, and response contracts

Facilities and equipment must be routinely inspected to prevent small problems from becoming catastrophes. Scheduled maintenance helps reduce the probability of major building and equipment failure. Once a problem is noted, immediate corrective action should be taken to prevent lengthy downtime or severe damage. A strong organizational safety program can reduce the incidence of accidental destruction or damage to records and information. Many employees do not consider records to be as important as productivity or machinery. Records and information management training programs are the best cures for employee misunderstanding or carelessness toward records and information.

Geographic location of the facility plays an important part in determining what precautions need to be taken. Heavy rainfall areas in close proximity to bodies of water may require extra flood precautions. Drought-prone areas demand enhanced fire safety practices. Areas with numerous incidents of hurricanes, tornadoes, or earthquakes will benefit from planned early warning drills.

Older buildings require more frequent maintenance and upkeep than new facilities. Wiring or plumbing may need to be inspected and repaired often or even replaced. Windows may not be seated properly to prevent leaking. Foundations may be cracked, or roofs may sag. Newer buildings may be constructed to minimum building codes and require extensive structural upgrading if a large volume of records or equipment is placed near the outer walls.

Building security requires adequate and effective means of fire, water or movement alarms, sound construction, human surveillance of entry and work areas, controlled access to buildings and work areas, and recorded monitoring of critical work sites or confidential records housing. Building security measures are not only necessary to reduce adverse consequences of a natural disaster, but they are also very important for preventing loss due to acts of terrorism or vandalism. In addition to protecting employee and customer lives, good building security is necessary for detecting potential threats and for diffusing the threat before a disaster can occur.

Security of records and information housing and storage facilities prevents theft, damage, and loss. Using common sense in storing inactive records protects vital information. NFPA 232, *Standard for the Protection of Records,* sets the standards for construction and rating of fire-resistant file cabinets, safes, and vaults, and sets the requirements for fire-resistant archives and records centers. The best building security, however, cannot fully protect records and information from an explosion or collapsed buildings. Many automated security programs are available to protect electronic information from theft or vandalism. Electronic records must also be protected from human error, carelessness, or deliberate destructiveness. Bear in mind that backup or replication of electronic data is only the first step in protecting data. The frequency, method, location of storage, and access to back-up or replicated data play a role in quickly restoring electronic information.

A loss prevention plan must also position the organization for immediate preparedness, response, and recovery when needed. Letting required contracts for response and recovery procedures must be done prior to the need for emergency preparedness. Letting contracts for items, such as recovery services, back-up generators, alternative operating sites, and emergency supplies, help speed response and recovery efforts. Vendors of these commodities and services usually require some type of contingency agreement or a retainer fee. A list of all contracted recovery and response vendors and any necessary equipment and supplies to be provided by the organization should be included in the emergency response plan.

Recovery services include a variety of assessment, salvage, and recovery operations. Many organizations prefer using recovery services for salvaging large volumes of records and information, recovery of specialized equipment, and restoring facilities to habitable conditions. Some requirements to consider when contracting for records and information recovery services include:

- What services does the vendor perform?
- Does the vendor provide all equipment and supplies to perform the services?
- Where is the vendor located and are branch offices or franchises located nearby?
- What is the average response time?
- Can the vendor call on resources outside the area if a community-wide disaster occurs?
- Is a retainer fee required?
- Does the retainer fee differ for faster response time or higher priority?
- Does the vendor perform or help perform the damage assessment?

- Does the vendor recover and restore all records and information media types?

- Will the vendor provide a price schedule for all services?

- What type of agreement or contract does the vendor require?

Alternative operating sites, sometimes combined with an alternative data source, are necessary following the destruction or inaccessibility of the normal work site. An **alternative operating site** is a secondary location or facility used to conduct critical business operations in the event of a disruptive event. Alternative sites can also include nontraditional options such as working from home (telecommuting) and mobile-office concepts. Some alternative sites are also used as command centers or operating centers during a community-wide event. Most alternative sites are classified as either a cold site or a hot site.

QUICK TIPS

- Make provisions for a cold site with computer environment. PCs and peripherals can be rented for the recovery phase.

- Team up with the contracted back-up storage provider to conduct disaster drills in order to reduce costs and still adequately test your disaster prevention plan.

A **cold site** is an alternative facility that has the necessary electrical and physical components of a computer facility, but does not have the computer equipment in place. The site is ready to receive the necessary replacement computer equipment in the event that the user has to move from their main computing location to an alternative site.[4] A cold site is less expensive than a hot site, but it takes longer to get an enterprise in full operation after the disaster. The location of the cold site should be far enough away to be operational during community-wide events but near enough to avoid prolonged travel time. Storing back-up tapes near the cold site can reduce recovery time.

A **hot site** is a fully operational offsite data processing facility equipped with hardware and system software to be used in the event of a disaster.[5] A business can use a hot site to continue computer and network operations in the event of a computer or equipment disruptive event. Hot sites may be a shared environment or a dedicated environment. Shared hot sites may have access limitations depending on how many organizations share the site and the type and extent of the event. Dedicated environments can be very expensive to maintain but may be within the risk tolerance of the organization.

QUICK TIP

Hot sites are more costly than cold sites.

"When calculating computer hot-site costs, compound them over 20 years to include the impact of the low probability of a disaster happening. It is not sufficient to cite only *annual* computer hot-site costs as a percentage of budget. And don't forget to compound the cost of money over the same period of time."

Source: Kenneth N. Myers, Business Continuity Strategies: Protecting Against Unplanned Disasters (New Jersey: John Wiley & Sons, 2006), 75.

If full restoration of the normal work site is estimated to be prolonged, contracts may be needed for both a cold site and a hot site. The organization can use the hot site until the cold site has been furnished with equipment. Typically, a business has an annual contract with a company that offers hot and cold site services with a monthly service charge. Some disaster recovery services offer back-up services so that all company data is available regardless of whether a hot site or cold site is used. If an enterprise must use a hot or cold site, daily fees and other incidental fees usually apply in addition to the basic service charge.

Alternative data sources, such as managed service providers or network storage environment duplication, are repositories used to house replicated data and information. A **managed service provider** is a contract service offering remote data protection services, including continuous online data backup, recovery, and electronic vaulting.

Network storage environment duplication includes storage area network (SAN) or network-attached storage (NAS). A **storage area network (SAN)** is a high-speed special-purpose network that interconnects different kinds of data storage devices with associated data servers. A storage area network can extend to remote locations for back-up and archival storage, using wide area network carrier technologies. SANs support mirroring, backup and restore, archival and retrieval of archived data, data migration from one storage device to another, and the sharing of data among different servers in a network. They can also incorporate with network-attached storage (NAS) systems.

Network-attached storage (NAS) is hard disk storage that is set up with its own network IP address on the organization's local area network (LAN) rather than being attached to the department server used for daily work applications. By removing storage access and its management from the department server, both application programming and files can be served faster because they are not competing for the same processor resources. File requests are mapped by the main server to the NAS file server. Network-attached storage consists of hard disk storage, including multidisk systems, and software for configuring and mapping file locations to the network-attached device.

With a well-developed and implemented loss prevention plan, recovering vital records and information is a simple process of retrieving the records and information and restoring them to the organization's files. Salvage efforts, when necessary, can then be directed toward the recovery of other important records and information.

A records and information loss prevention plan should contain the following items:

- The vital records matrix

- Compiled results of the risk management processes

- Procedures for eliminating, mitigating, and monitoring potential hazards to the records and information

- Copies of current ongoing mitigation and response and recovery contracts, and the names, addresses, and communication numbers of vendor contacts

Test and Update the Loss Prevention Plan

A loss prevention plan is a dynamic, changing document requiring ongoing review and improvement to assure adequate protection and timely recovery of vital information. Specific procedures should include maintaining a continuous and timely update of identified vital records and methods of protection. This internal audit and update procedure should be coordinated with any review and update of the emergency management or business continuity plan.

A loss prevention plan is only effective if it reflects the current operating environment and critical functions of the organization. The plan must be periodically reviewed, tested, and updated. Some key factors that trigger a periodic review, test, and update process are:

- New vital records matrixes, new information processing equipment, and new communications systems

- New electronic records and information applications and service providers

- New organizational operating locations

- Major changes to facility structure or layout

- Changes in facility or community vulnerabilities; e.g., the discovery of a previously unknown hazardous waste dump near an organization's facility, or the discovery of asbestos in the ceiling insulation of the records storage area

This periodic review ensures effective maintenance of a loss prevention plan. Initially, the review

DISASTER SNAPSHOT

On April 14, 2010, drifting ash from an erupting volcano in Iceland caused a massive aviation crisis in Europe. In the following weeks, almost 100,000 flights were canceled, causing stranded passengers throughout Europe. The effects of the volcanic eruption also highlighted the reality that, in today's interconnected and globalized economy, just one disruptive event can significantly impact the flow of business operations around the world. Public and private sector organizations all over the world depend on air traffic to and from the European continent to deliver key functions to their stakeholders. Military agencies, businesses, and individuals from all sectors felt the ripple effect on the critical European transportation hub shutdown.

Corporations worldwide were forced to make critical decisions and hold meetings while key employees and executives were stranded around the globe and rely on methods of instant communication. Alternative methods of product and service delivery had to be immediately implemented. The event pointed out the need for preparing for crises that will affect the organization indirectly. Strategies are needed not only to respond to local or regional disruptive events, but also to enact planned responses when employees are stranded due to regional disruptive events in their locations.

Source: Kenneth N. Myers, *Business Continuity Strategies: Protecting Against Unplanned Disasters* (New Jersey: John Wiley & Sons, 2006), 75.

should be conducted three times a year. Later, unless necessity demands it, the review can be performed annually. "The organization's original assessment of its vulnerabilities is the basis on which its first emergency management or business continuity plan is founded. The plan must be changed, therefore, to conform to the revised evaluation of these dangers."[5]

An essential mechanism necessary for ensuring that the loss prevention plan is current is an emergency management or business continuity manual. The policy, procedure, and responsibilities sections of the manual should be revised as changes occur.

Testing the loss prevention plan is essential to the success of the procedures during disaster recovery activation. Testing can demonstrate weaknesses in the functionality of the plan and in employee training and awareness. Emergency response plan testing is discussed in detail in Chapter 6.

Vital records program and risk management processes become a part of the loss prevention plan. The loss prevention plan, in turn, becomes a part of the emergency management or business continuity plan.

In 1993, the World Trade Center was bombed. Immediately following the bombing, all evacuation plans were reviewed. As a result, evacuation routes received enhanced lighting; additional fire wardens were identified, trained, and placed on each floor of the center; and the periodicity of fire drills was increased.

Lesson Learned

"An efficient time to review revisions is after tests have been made, because they too must be performed periodically and because they often reveal omissions, improved controls and methods, and matters that are not clear."[6]

CHAPTER 5 CHECKLIST

Loss Prevention Plan

☐ Develop a clear loss prevention policy.

☐ Monitor relevancy of prevention, response, and recovery contracts.

☐ Establish procedures for monitoring potential hazards and destructive forces.

☐ Establish employee training program.

☐ Establish procedures for ongoing review and revision.

Prepare and Implement the Loss Prevention Plan

☐ Establish activities necessary to reduce or eliminate existing hazards as identified by the risk management process.

☐ Establish employee training program to prevent human error, unsafe work procedures, or carelessness.

☐ Establish procedures for frequent building and equipment inspections and proper maintenance.

☐ Implement building security measures.

☐ Implement an information security program.

☐ Let prevention, recovery, and response contracts.

Test and Update the Loss Prevention Plan

☐ Test the plan.

☐ Establish periodic updating of the loss prevention plan.

NOTES

1. Kenneth N. Myers, *Business Continuity Strategies: Protecting Against Unplanned Disasters* (Hoboken: John Wiley & Sons, Inc., 2006), 147.

2. Joanne E. Hurd, "Do You Know Where the Briefcase Is?" *Journal of Systems Management* 3X/400 45, no. 8 (August 1994): 18.

3. Hurd, "Do You Know Where the Briefcase Is?," 18.

4. National Institute of Standards and Technology, SP800-34, *Contingency Planning Guide for Information Technology Systems* (June 2002), E-1, E-2.

5. Ken Doughty, *Business Continuity Planning: Protect Your Organization's Life* (CRC Press LLC, 2001), 367.

6. Doughty, *Business Continuity Planning*, 367.

SECTION III:
PREPAREDNESS

Preparedness involves the activities that develop records and information capabilities for the operational response to an emergency. The primary preparedness activity is the preparation of a *records and information emergency response plan*. Section III includes information on preparing, implementing, updating, and testing the emergency response plan.

Prepare a Records and Information Emergency Management Plan

"Your plan should become a living document, never finally done, but changing as your organization grows and changes."[1]

The **preparedness phase** involves the activities that develop records and information capabilities for operational response to an emergency and continuity of the organization following a disruptive event. The purpose of emergency or business continuity planning is to provide the basis for systematic responses to disruptive events that threaten an organization and the records and information necessary for continuing operations. Survival is not just getting through the immediate event. Survival also means maintaining the competitive position and financial stability of an organization immediately following and continuing long after a disruptive event.

The primary preparedness activity is the preparation of a records and information emergency response plan. An **emergency response plan** is a documented plan addressing the immediate reaction and response to an emergency situation.[2] It is a compilation of procedures and policies designed to guide the organization through a disruptive event, including the assets involved, the mitigation steps taken, and specific actions to be taken should an event occur. A well-designed plan can significantly minimize the organization's potential loss.

Both an emergency response plan and a business continuity plan are used to deploy the full range of available response measures to a disruptive event. Records and information play a role in the overall plan, but do not have priority during response or recovery. Safety and preservation of life are the foremost goals of response plans.

Planning Team

The team approach recommended in Chapter 2 as a means to obtain management support can serve as a mechanism for the development and implementation of the emergency response or business continuity plan. The team organized to prepare the emergency management or business continuity management proposal can also serve as the core of the response planning team. Its size and composition depend upon the timeline associated with the project. At its earliest stage, a smaller team is recommended. This core team, at this stage, lays the foundation for the plan. As the project progresses, add other key individuals to the team. A multitiered team, comprised of executives, managers, front-line supervisors, and subject matter experts, ensures a cross-functional planning team.

The team leader, often referred to as the *contingency planning coordinator* or *business continuity manager,* is integral to the overall success of the plan. This individual must keep the plan's objectives in focus.

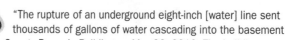

DISASTER SNAPSHOT

"The rupture of an underground eight-inch [water] line sent thousands of gallons of water cascading into the basement of the Dallas County Records Building on May 30, 2010. The building, dating back to 1922, houses some of the county's oldest records, including deeds to properties." County offices had to go back to using manual processes to conduct county business. Procedures, such as issuing marriage licenses and birth certificates and filing probate records, were temporarily diverted to other nearby counties. The main county tax office at the Records Building was closed, but tax offices in the nine sub-courthouses were available for motor vehicle registration and license plates and titles.

Workers from various county departments housed in the building could not return to their offices until June 28. Electrical panels in the basement of the Records Building, dating to the 1920s, were inundated by the six feet of water covering the basement after the break. Costs of repairs and cleanup were over $10 million. Most of the damage was covered by insurance, but the county was liable for a $1 million deductible.

In 2008, County Commissioners hired a consultant to form a plan for a computer backup and review of the county's entire information technology needs. Unfortunately, the committee established to implement the plan was dissolved by the committee six months later because they said, "It didn't move quickly after the consultant concluded [that] the county needed a back-up system. As a result, commissioners didn't arrange for a back-up system in case of a disaster, and county computers went down for most of a week.

Sources: "Flooding of Dallas records office 'catastrophic,' say officials," by Cynthia Vega and Brad Watson, WFAA, Dallas, Texas (Posted 1 June 2010 at 7:31 a.m.; Updated Tuesday, 1 June at 5:21 p.m.). 5 March 2011 <*http://www.wfaa.com/news/local/Dallas-records—95886509.html*>.

Budget Considerations and Cost Estimation

If emergency management or business continuity planning activities are not performed and a disruptive event occurs, the organization may suffer unacceptable losses. When an organization suffers losses, it negatively affects the organization's resources, which, in turn, affects customers. Product or service delays, inconveniences, and possible price increases to recoup losses will occur. If emergency management or business continuity planning activities are implemented, the organization must absorb the cost of these activities and may pass those costs on to their customers. Like mitigation, the amount of preparation an organization is willing to pay for depends on its risk tolerance. However, an incomplete plan may result in more costly response and recovery and possibly irretrievable losses.

As with most planning projects, expenditure of resources begs the question: Is payback possible? **Payback** is that point in time when an organization's investment, or cash outlay, is returned in the form of a benefit. Payback is not always a desirable effect of emergency or business continuity management. In order for payback to occur, the organization would have to be involved in a disruptive event and be successful at mitigating loss. With all four phases of emergency and business continuity management in place, mitigating loss is feasible; therefore, payback is only achieved following successful recovery from a disruptive event.

An organization cannot predict an event. However, based on the geographic location, the organization can make some reasonable assumptions about event probabilities. California and earthquakes, Florida and hurricanes, or Kansas and tornados are but a few examples of locations where a disaster probability may be higher than others. However, probabilities are not accurate predictions of potential payback. Regardless of the event, the organization will incur costs for responding to and recovering from a disruptive event. Planning for those costs ahead of time is essential to successful response and recovery.

Estimate Costs

The lower the probability of a disruptive event occurring, the greater the search should be for the lowest-cost solution. Economically, the level of resources necessary for resolution of an event that may *never* occur should not equal those necessary for resolution of an event of high probability. Embedding this cost-control philosophy from the onset ensures a continual search for cost-effective solutions. Using the probability and impact matrix discussed in Chapter 3 combined with estimated costs for each potential action can greatly assist in determining the probable cost of an event and any loss suffered during and after the event.

During a disruptive event, the organization that loses revenue because of a shutdown considers the loss of revenue as an expense. Keeping this in mind, determining the financial effect a disruptive event may have on the organization should not be difficult. Calculate operations and production shutdown losses by using the potential revenues, expenses, and net profit for a normal day. Couple this with the potential cost of recovery activities, and other losses from the event, such as destroyed facilities or vital records and information losses, and the financial reversal for the event can be determined.

The financial reversal with an effective emergency management or business continuity plan in place would be considerably less than with no plan or an incomplete plan, even after factoring in the cost of mitigation and response.

Similar calculations can be made in planning the financial picture for any organization and any known scenarios can be played out, as discussed later in this chapter. Funding for equipment, materials, supplies, and labor also can be projected. As the planning phase of emergency or business continuity management progresses, the organization should keep financial planning a priority.

Determine Response and Recovery Strategies

When recovering interrupted operations, the organization should attempt to reach past the point at which it will just survive and should set a recovery time objective that gives it a margin in case of unforeseen difficulties with recovery. Continuity and recovery capabilities must be realistic and within an acceptable maximum tolerable period of disruption. The **maximum tolerable period of disruption (MTPD)** is the timeframe during which a recovery must become effective before an outage compromises the ability of an organization to achieve its business objectives and/or survival. Activating a hot site or reconstructing the operating system and data on a server may take more time than expected. Allow sufficient time for continuity and recovery to ensure that business activities can be resumed within an established recovery time objective. A **recovery time objective (RTO)** is the time by which mission-critical activities and/or their dependencies must be recovered.[3] An organization must set a reasonable maximum tolerable period of disruption and an achievable recovery time objective in order to effectively continue in business following an event. Both the maximum tolerable period of disruption and the recovery time objective will affect the acceptable risk tolerance level of the organization.

The process of establishing a response strategy should include:[4]

- Using the results from the business impact analysis, note the acceptable maximum tolerable period of disruption.

- Deciding on a recovery time objective for the product or service, which should (of course) be shorter than the maximum tolerable period of disruption.

- Conducting a 'gap analysis' to identify where existing performance is measured against the required performance—if a resumption strategy currently exists.

- Providing executive management with a strategic evaluation.

- Ensuring that executive management signs off on the agreed option, including the financial and resource provisions.

Response to a disruptive event includes those activities occurring immediately before, during, or immediately after the event. Response execution responsibilities must be identified and delegated as part of the emergency response plan. The response strategy should include all loss prevention methods for access to and recovery of records and information (discussed in Chapter 5) including:

- Establishing contracts, policy, and procedures for use of alternative sites and alternative access to managed service providers.
- Establishing responsibilities for execution of response measures and tasks, including those listed on the vital records matrix.
- Determining and securing access to external resources.
- Establishing procedures for restoring systems.
- Determining necessary response support documents (V1 records).

All emergencies generally require basic common sense response resources. Among these are employee and vendor contact information, facility access contact data, and equipment listings. Additionally, inventories of the organization's vital records, software applications, and communications are necessary.

Sort the collected data, segregating the contact information. As contact information is subject to frequent updates, maintain it in a separate document. Organize the remaining data for compilation into a comprehensive manual.

The plan should cover all possible events. Plan for some common disruptive events, including:

- Fire
- Hazardous materials incidents
- Floods and flash floods
- Hurricanes
- Tornadoes
- Severe winter storms
- Earthquakes
- Technological emergencies[5]
- Pandemic influenza outbreaks

Document the Plan

Once the overall foundation of the plan has been laid and the response strategy determined, documenting it is relatively easy. The sample emergency plan depicted in Figure 6.1 provides a step-by-step guide suitable for use by an organization of any size.

Policy Statement

A key written element of the plan is its policy statement that should include the purpose of the plan and the goals and objectives and the means to reach them; anticipated benefits that the organization will gain by plan accomplishment; the scope of the plan, to whom it applies, and the overall impacts of plan accomplishment; and the plan components and statements of policy and legal authority. Clarify timelines, success criteria, and expectations.

Responsibilities and Authority

The plan must specifically list the positions designated to activate the plan as well as under what conditions those designated positions are authorized to trigger the plan's activation. The response team and their responsibilities must also be defined in detail. Records and information response and recovery responsibilities include those listed on the vital records matrix.

Task Organization

Organizational size may dictate that several teams be involved in plan development and documentation activities. If several teams are involved, each team and respective member responsibilities should

---

Emergency Management Plan Components

Policy Statement

☐ State purpose of the plan; means to reach the goals and objectives.

☐ State goals and objectives; benefits the organization will gain by plan accomplishment.

☐ State scope of the plan; to whom it applies and overall impacts of plan accomplishment.

☐ List plan components; statements of policy and legal authority.

Responsibilities and Authority

☐ State position(s) with overall authority.

☐ List responsibilities of essential positions.

☐ List position responsible for plan maintenance and distribution.

☐ Describe overall responsibilities of employees.

Task Organization

☐ Outline chief coordinator's duties and responsibilities.

☐ Outline response team's duties and responsibilities.

☐ Outline recovery team's duties and responsibilities.

☐ Outline damage assessment team's duties and responsibilities.

☐ Designate other assigned teams or key positions.

Communication Procedures

☐ Establish formal verbal communication linkages; primary and secondary.

☐ Establish formal written communication linkages; primary and secondary.

☐ Develop and list communication alternatives.

☐ Develop information transport policy, procedure, and contingency.

Preparedness Checklists

☐ Develop preparedness steps for each event scenario based on the risk analysis.

☐ Categorize checklists based on the three types of emergencies: natural, technological, and social.

☐ Segregate the four phases of emergency management; however,

    ☐ Integrate efforts and results with the other phases.

Response Checklists

☐ Develop response steps for each event scenario based on the risk analysis.

☐ Categorize checklists based on the three types of emergencies: natural, technological, and social.

☐ Segregate the four phases of emergency management; however,

    ☐ Integrate efforts and results with the other phases.

Recovery Checklists

☐ Develop recovery steps for each event scenario based on the risk analysis.

☐ Categorize checklists based on the three types of emergencies: natural, technological, and social.

☐ Segregate the four phases of emergency management; however,

    ☐ Integrate efforts and results with the other phases.

Training Programs

☐ Establish goals and objectives for training all employees.

☐ Develop specific training programs for event responders.

☐ Develop specific training programs for specialized teams.

☐ Develop a plan for training personnel outside the organization who have a role.

Figure 6.1 Sample Emergency Management Plan Components (continued on page 68)

Emergency Management Plan Components (continued)

Testing Procedures

☐ Establish goals and objectives for conducting exercises based on event scenarios.

☐ Develop schedule and plan for conducting tabletop exercises.

☐ Develop schedule and plan for conducting functional exercises.

☐ Develop schedule and plan for conducting full-scale exercises.

Review and Update Responsibilities

☐ Develop goals and objectives to ensure plan remains current.

☐ Establish a team to help with review and update activities.

☐ Establish a schedule for routine maintenance of the plan.

☐ Establish procedures to collect data from real or simulated events for plan modification.

Communications Directory

☐ Employee work and home telephone numbers

☐ Employee physical and email addresses (emergency personnel)

☐ Listing of emergency call hierarchy

☐ Inventory of essential equipment

☐ Inventory of communications equipment

☐ Listing of key municipal agencies and contacts

☐ Maps of area

☐ Listing of pertinent customers

☐ Facility telephone numbers/addresses

☐ Fax numbers and email addresses for vendors/contractors

☐ Vendor telephone numbers/addresses

☐ Listing of local utility companies

☐ Listing of hospitals and care facilities

☐ Listing of television, radio, and newspaper telephone numbers/addresses

Continuity or Succession of Authority

☐ Establish a plan to continue organization leadership if current leadership becomes incapacitated.

☐ Establish clear lines of authority in the succession hierarchy.

☐ Establish clear policy for duration and extent of authority.

☐ Establish multiple strategies for re-establishing authority (contingency plan).

Damage Assessment

☐ Develop damage assessment policy and procedures.

☐ Develop strategy for addressing both initial damage assessment and post-disaster activities.

☐ Develop guideline for relationship with local government emergency coordinators.

☐ Develop necessary forms to record damage assessment information.

Financial or Funding Information

☐ Establish guidelines for emergency fund withdrawals.

☐ Establish emergency fund account codes to track expenditures.

☐ Establish policy and procedures for the emergency petty cash funds.

☐ Establish auditing policy and procedures to ensure accountability.

Figure 6.1 Sample Emergency Management Plan Components

be included in the plan. If citizen or other corporate partners are included in the emergency process, list them in the plan. Various teams that may be involved include:

1. *Disaster Decision-Making Team*
   - Notifies board of directors, regulatory bodies, and media as required.
   - Makes final decisions for activation of the emergency management plan.
   - Makes major expenditure and funding-related decisions.

2. *Steering Committee*
   - Establishes policies and procedures.
   - Defines the plans structure to ensure cohesiveness of teams.
   - Serves as a facilitator should a disaster occur, notifies affected personnel, secures the affective areas, and ensures that individuals involved in the recovery effort have basic necessities.

3. *Management Operations Team*
   - Coordinates all emergency operations teams from the business resumption site.
   - Determines the extent of the disaster.
   - Forwards requests for supplies, equipment, and additional personnel to department coordinators Team.
   - Monitors progress of emergency operations team.

4. *Department Coordinators Team*
   - Composed of members from each functional area.
   - Communicates the status and needs of each respective department.
   - Notifies emergency operations team managers of the disaster occurrence.
   - Coordinates recovery efforts.
   - Processes requests for required resources.

5. *Emergency Operations Team*
   - Facilitates smooth transition to emergency back-up center.
   - Notifies key personnel and affected families.
   - Monitors adherence to and effectiveness of emergency procedures.
   - Processes requests for mail or courier service, replacement software, and back-up power.

6. *Damage Assessment and Post-Investigation Team*
   - Informs management operations team of the extent of damage.
   - Investigates cause of disaster.

7. *Reconstruction Team*
   - Composed of positions required for restoration of the damaged area.
   - Coordinates temporary and long-term reconstruction efforts.

Communication Procedures

The plan should include methods for employees' and responders' communication if a disruptive event occurs. Establish formal primary and secondary verbal and written communication linkages. Determine whether landline telephones, cellphones, radios, or other methods of communication are to be used and which employees will use them. Define which information will be hand delivered, where information will be delivered, and how information will be delivered. For example, emergency or vital records and information may need to be transferred to a requestor via a special color-coded mail pouch or over secure server connections.

Preparedness Checklist

The plan must address specific events and identify which procedures and tasks are required to respond to them. It must provide for both major events (such as a hurricane) and minor events (such as a breach of personal data), and it should include both site-specific and community-wide events. Organizations should have a checklist covering each type of event and the steps necessary to prepare for and control the emergency. A sample checklist for a step-by-step process of securing vital records and information, computer-related equipment, and vendor contact listings for hurricane response is shown in Figure 6.2.

Hurricane Preparedness, Response, and Recovery Checklist

PREPAREDNESS

Condition 5 – Beginning of Hurricane Season, June 1

All Functions:

- ☐ Review hurricane response plan and provide updates.
- ☐ Attend hurricane staff meetings as directed.
- ☐ Review essential personnel listings. *(Ref: Emergency Communications Directory)*
- ☐ Review and inventory emergency supplies.
- ☐ Ensure that equipment is maintained in optimal condition.

Records Management Function:

- ☐ Train response team.
- ☐ Establish/maintain emergency fund for supply purchases.
- ☐ Verify operation of recovery equipment.
- ☐ Update hurricane response plan as needed.
- ☐ Establish or verify contracts for alternative access to information and for recovery service.
- ☐ Verify availability of contingency storage.

Condition 4 – 72-Hour Alert

All Functions:

- ☐ Review emergency plans and procedures.
- ☐ Place essential personnel on Condition 4 alert and brief on storm.
- ☐ Track and log all activities and expenditures associated with the storm.

Records Management Function:

- ☐ Meet with records management emergency coordinators to review plan.
- ☐ Establish contact with offsite contingency records storage center to inform of need for storm storage.
- ☐ Establish contact with alternative site and inform of possible activation.

RESPONSE

Condition 3 – 48 Hours: Hurricane "Watch"

All Functions:

- ☐ Activate full emergency plan status as deemed appropriate.
- ☐ Assemble response team and review plan.
- ☐ Initiate FEMA recordkeeping for hours and materials.
- ☐ Call recovery vendors to check availability for work after storm.

Records Management Function:

- ☐ Prepare to establish electronic data access and equipment at command center.
- ☐ Request backup of all electronic files; have users label and secure for contingency storage.

Figure 6.2 Sample Hurricane Preparedness, Response, and Recovery Checklist (continued on page 71)

Hurricane Preparedness, Response, and Recovery Checklist (continued)

Condition 2 – 24 Hours: Hurricane "Warning"

All Functions:

☐ Move emergency response equipment to designated locations.

☐ Brief recovery staff and crews as to where and when they are to report.

☐ Secure equipment.

☐ Track and log all activities and expenditures associated with the storm.

Records Management Function:

☐ Secure records and information equipment.

☐ Restore electronic applications and required data at command center.

☐ Secure physical V1 records and move to command center.

☐ Collect all vital and back-up records to be housed at offsite contingency storage center.

☐ Secure all nonvital paper records—move off work surfaces and into lockable file drawers or overheads.

Condition 1 – 12 Hours or Less: Evacuation

All Functions:

☐ Designate response personnel to complete setup of command center and satellite facilities (fill water jugs, test equipment, check communications, set up first aid).

☐ Shut down all nonessential equipment.

☐ Continue to track and log all activities and expenditures associated with the storm.

Records Management Function:

☐ Establish a time to reconvene communications (Recovery Phase).

☐ Send all vital and back-up records to offsite contingency storage center.

Condition 0 – Landfall

All Functions:

☐ Take safety precautions. Personal safety is a priority.

☐ Continue to track and log all activities and expenditures associated with the storm.

☐ Maintain contact with command center and satellite centers.

☐ Provide frequent briefings to work crews and other essential personnel.

RECOVERY

All Functions:

☐ Relieve response personnel within 12 hours or as directed.

☐ Start damage assessment of facilities; prepare initial damage assessment (IDA) reports.

☐ Evaluate planning and preparedness efforts.

☐ Continue to track and log all activities and expenditures associated with the storm.

Records Management Function:

☐ Relocate electronic equipment as deemed appropriate and establish electronic data access.

☐ Activate recovery service as needed.

☐ Secure recovery areas to ensure no further damage to records and information.

☐ Contact offsite contingency storage center to deliver vital and back-up records to operating site.

☐ Contact alternative site as needed for activation.

Figure 6.2 Sample Hurricane Preparedness, Response, and Recovery Checklist

Response Checklist

Include a response checklist for each event listed in the plan. These steps should be continuous or sequential from the preparedness phase to the response phase for each emergency addressed. The vital records matrix and records recovery priority lists should be included.

Additionally, disaster recovery procedures, disaster recovery services and resources, and salvage equipment and supply listings should also be included. The plan should show when an emergency status is upgraded from one phase to the next. A response checklist is similar to the preparedness checklist (see Figure 6.2). A sample checklist for responding to a breach of personal data is shown in Figure 6.3.

Data Breach Response Checklist[6]

Employee
- ☐ Detects a data breach or is informed of a breach.
- ☐ Notifies their supervisor and/or manager (as applicable).
- ☐ Supervisor or manager notifies IT manager.

Information Technology
- ☐ Receives notice of or discovers breach incident. A suspected or identified breach may be reported to IT by any manager.
- ☐ Records management begins entry into the data breach log.
- ☐ Notifies CEO and appropriate departmental manager.

If an IT breach:
- ☐ Takes appropriate corrective action(s).
- ☐ Notifies concerned parties that it is corrected.
- ☐ Makes appropriate log entries as actions are completed.
- ☐ Monitors corrective action(s) for continued security.

Departmental Representative
- ☐ Makes ongoing appropriate entries into the data breach log.
- ☐ Notifies and discloses to corporate counsel that a breach of personally identifiable information has taken place.
- ☐ Notifies and discloses to the appropriate law enforcement agency and corporate counsel—if the breach of personal information is deemed to be criminal in scope—that a breach has occurred and provided the known details of the breach.
- ☐ Waits for notification from corporate counsel or law enforcement agency before proceeding—in cases of criminal intent.
- ☐ Prepares a notification letter containing:
  - The incident in general terms.
  - The type of personal information that was subject to the unauthorized access and acquisition.
  - The general acts of the company to protect the personal information from further unauthorized access.
  - A telephone number that the person may call for further information and assistance.
  - Advice that directs the person to remain vigilant by reviewing account statements and monitoring free credit reports.
- ☐ Generates the notification letter and mails (or emails when appropriate) to everyone impacted by the breach of information after determining that the notification will not or no longer impede the investigation or jeopardize national or homeland security.
- ☐ Notifies corporate counsel and all consumer reporting agencies that compile and maintain files on consumers on a nationwide basis, where required, as defined in 15 U.S.C. §1681a(p), of the timing, distribution, and content of the notice.
- ☐ Completes appropriate entries into the data breach log.

Figure 6.3 Sample Data Breach Response Checklist

Recovery Checklist

A recovery checklist should also show the continuing steps from the response phase to the recovery phase. The response checklist should indicate brief statements regarding particular activities that should be performed in the recovery phase. A recovery checklist is similar to the preparedness and response checklists (see Figure 6.2).

Training Programs

Employees cannot follow the plan appropriately if they have not received training in how to use it. At a minimum, response personnel should have annual training on plan contents. A training program outline should be included in the plan to document the topics on which employees have been trained and the frequency that the training was administered. Training requirements should be updated annually or after each revision to the plan. If the resources to conduct training do not exist in-house, training should be outsourced to professionals.

Testing Procedures

The plan must include goals, objectives, and schedules for conducting exercises or simulations. Specific types of exercises to be used for the most likely disruptive events should also be in the plan. Types of exercises are discussed in detail later in this chapter.

Review and Update Responsibilities

The plan requires periodic review and revision to remain effective when a disruptive event occurs. This plan should be revised as necessary and thoroughly revised at least annually.

Communications Directory

Communication information collected by the planning team when developing the plan should be included as a separate annex or appendix of the plan. The information contains a variety of names (individual and company), telephone and cellphone numbers, addresses (including email), and inventories. Because this information changes frequently and because some contact information may be considered private, the lists should be separated from the rest of the plan. Separate lists will allow better security of the personal data and easier updating. Job titles are usually appropriate to reference in the plan itself when referring to individual positions.

Continuity or Succession of Authority

In the event that the organization loses one or more of its leaders in a disaster, remaining executives should be prepared to assign temporary authority. The planning team should include a clear statement of the chain of authority and composition of a crisis team, including alternates, when key officers are unavailable. Figure 6.4 contains a sample statement assigning the chain of authority during an emergency.

Succession of Authority Resolution

The Board of Directors, during its regular meeting, proposed, discussed, and unanimously approved that:

In the event of a major disaster (as defined in the emergency response plan) in which the Chief Executive Officer and his/her assistant are killed or shall be unavailable, the direction of this corporation shall automatically pass, in descending order, to the following senior officers: Vice President of Operations, Vice President of Public Relations, and Chief Legal Counsel. The senior surviving officer shall immediately gather or appoint at least four additional officers to assist in managing the corporation during the crisis period.

The Board of Directors, at the earliest opportunity, shall confirm all actions of the emergency response team and elect a new chief executive and senior officers.

The policy was approved at a meeting of the Board of Directors on January 1, 2011.

Figure 6.4 Sample Succession of Authority Resolution

Damage Assessment

Plans should include specific guidance for assessing damage and reporting it to the appropriate authority. **Damage assessment** includes assigning a team to assess the damage immediately following a disaster, documenting damage to organizational assets, and reporting the findings to the proper authority. Reports could be submitted to an insurance company, the local emergency management director, and/or FEMA.

Financial or Funding Information

Emergency response plans should include guidance for handling funding. The organization may need to purchase equipment and supplies for responding to or recovering from disruptive events. Additionally, finance and accounting personnel need to track expenses associated with an event. Establish specific codes for labor, equipment, and supplies to ensure proper accounting of expenses. Funding planning should include start-up costs such as estimated personnel expenses, estimated operational expenses, and estimated material and supply expenses, plan maintenance costs, and a contingency fund.

QUICK TIP

Many small business owners lease space in shopping centers or malls. The owner or manager of the center or mall may assist businesses in developing emergency management plans. After all, when businesses have undertaken preventive measures and are prepared for emergency situations, the facility owner benefits as well.

Start-up Costs

Calculating start-up costs related to plan development requires some thought as to how the plan development process will be handled. Personnel costs (including benefits), operational expenses, and material and supply expenses must be included in start-up costs.

1. *Personnel expenses.* Calculating personnel expenses depends on how the organization's resources will be applied to the development effort. In most organizations, personnel are a major expense and therefore the response plan should limit required personnel to only those essential to response and recovery. In addition, the organization must include benefits costs when determining personnel expenses.

2. *Operational expenses.* In calculating costs to develop an emergency response plan for records and information, operational expenses (i.e., those expenses associated with utilities, contracts, equipment or leases, and insurances) must also be considered. Specific examples of operational expenses include: telephone costs, electrical costs, facility lease costs, cost of copy and fax machines, cost of computer equipment rental, and percentage of costs of vehicles used for traveling to gather information. Certain operational expenses may be associated with the facility designated as the emergency response site and alternative operational and recovery sites. A command site or control center may need to be established prior to or during an event to manage emergency response activities. Additional expenses are associated with the establishment of this facility.

   Other operational expenses related to facilities include detection devices. Detection devices or systems are important to ensure early warning and control over disruptive events. Losses can be reduced or greatly mitigated if these devices or systems are installed. Examples of detection devices include motion, heat, humidity, smoke, leak, and chemical sensors. The plan should address inspection, maintenance, testing, and calibration of the detection devices.[7] Employees should know where the devices are located, and they should be trained to recognize neglect or abuse of the devices. In the U.S., all detection devices must have audible and visual alarm capabilities that comply with the current Americans with Disabilities Act (ADA).

   If insurance policies are reviewed and modified, include any additional costs (or savings) in operational costs. Additionally, if any phase of the plan is contracted to outside suppliers, the amounts should be added to the operational expenses. These contracts could be for recovery or salvage, managed service providers, alternative sites, vital records storage, or any other applicable emergency response activity.

3. *Material and supply expenses.* All material and supply expenses should be included in the total start-up costs for plan development. Material and supply expenses may include paper and supplies for general plan development, plywood for boarding up windows, spare computer supplies, boxes for records, plastic for covering records, flashlights, batteries, first-aid kits, and anything else purchased and set aside for the emergency response process. Sources and alternative sources for procuring materials and supplies should be established. Record the approximate expenses for the items and the waiting time between order placement and delivery.

Each member of the response team should assemble and maintain a personal supply kit containing clothing, equipment, and personal items that will be needed during the first 18 hours of a recovery operation. Persons who may be called upon to respond to disasters outside the area will require personal supplies for a minimum of 72 hours.

The personal supply kit should meet individual needs. A day pack or duffle bag may be an appropriate container. The kit should be assembled before the event alert. When alerted for an emergency response operation, employees are expected to report to the designated site within the hour. Clothing should be comfortable and suited for the current weather conditions.

Employees will probably be working under poor conditions, and the environment probably will be wet and dirty. Employees may be working outside or in an unheated building. If special protective clothing, such as a HazMat suit, is required and furnished by the employer, the cost of this clothing should be considered a material-and-supply expense by the organization.

Every organization is different in some respects; therefore, customized worksheets or checklists will help personnel procure the materials and supplies needed for an event. A sample list of supplies for records and information recovery is shown in Figure 6.5.

Basic Supply List
Records and Information Recovery

This list is designed to provide some of the basic supplies needed for the first 24 hours of a salvage operation. At least one of every item should be in inventory and secured in a safe place.

1. Locked fire-resistant safe to hold the following documents:
   • Copy of the emergency management plan
   • Configuration and priority plan for electronic data and applications restoration
   • Vital records matrix

2. Waterproof box to hold the following supplies:
   • Plastic sheeting
   • Ball of twine
   • Scissors
   • Rubber gloves
   • Batteries for camera, flashlight, and radio (one set for each item)
   • Waterproof pens
   • Extra memory cards for digital camera
   • Battery-operated radio
   • Flashlight
   • Adhesive labels (waterproof)
   • Name tags and colored adhesive labels for identification
   • Notebooks for documentation/ clipboards
   • Filament tape
   • Freezer paper
   • Paper towels and sponges
   • Plastic rulers or paint stirrers
   • Plastic bags to house wet microfilm, CDs, or DVDs
   • Plastic trash bags
   • Heavy duty, waterproof extension cords(s)
   • Mono filament line

Figure 6.5 Basic Records and Information Recovery Supply List

Plan Maintenance Costs

Although predicting costs associated with an actual disruptive event is difficult, estimating and budgeting for ongoing plan maintenance is possible. **Plan maintenance costs** associated with a program accrue after the program has been implemented and are reoccurring. Many costs associated with start-up can be used to determine ongoing costs. For example, many supplies have to be purchased initially; however, an annual inventory may result in the necessity to replenish or replace some supply items.

Once the plan is developed and implemented, personnel should consider routine maintenance costs associated with keeping the plan current and useful. Specific requirements will vary with each organization. However, plan maintenance costs usually include annual training, updating the written plan, testing or exercising the plan, purchasing perishable supplies, personnel costs to maintain the plan, storage costs for emergency supplies, emergency contract renewal, and equipment replacements.

Contingency Fund

Identifying the resources to mitigate or reduce the effects of a disruptive event can require very detailed planning. The more effective the planning efforts, the more likely financial resources will be available to aid in recovering from an event.

As planning efforts result in documented steps to deal with events and back-up or contingency arrangements are established, funding must also be included to ensure that the plan can be successfully activated. To supplement insurance and other financial resources, a contingency fund should be established to ensure that financial resources are available when needed. If the organization qualifies for FEMA resources, it must follow the strict reporting guidelines and procedures required by FEMA.

In the U.S., FEMA may also decide, based on the scope of the disaster and financial situation of the individual or organization, whether to allow a grant or to refer the applicant to a loan agency for assistance. For example, the U.S. Small Business Administration (SBA) is involved in disaster assistance and can offer loans to qualified organizations. If serious financial considerations exist, the SBA can refer applicants to the Individual and Family Grant (IFG) program. Under this program, grants are offered to seriously affected applicants.[8]

Having a contingency fund established when planning for disruptive events is important for the continued operation of the organization. If an event occurs, insurance, a small business loan, or a grant may be the primary means of getting the organization back into operation. However, to ensure that the organization has enough cash and immediate access to cash following an event, a contingency fund is needed.

Approve the Plan and Train Personnel

The completed draft emergency response plan needs to be approved by the governing board or commission and upper management. The planning team should meet with the appropriate levels of management and present and discuss the draft plan. Although management should be involved from the beginning and know what efforts have gone into the plan, their final approval will formalize the plan.

When the final plan is ready for distribution, all employees should be informed of the plan and appropriate employees should be trained. Appropriate personnel should conduct formal training sessions to educate them on the various plan elements. Participants who complete the training should sign a training roster that provides proof of training for legal purposes.

Review and Update the Plan

Planning and response teams must constantly review and update the plan. They must quickly integrate new elements of the total records and information program into the plan. Introduction of new computer hardware or applications, the development of additional vital records for a new product or service, a change in accounting procedures, or the conversion of paper records to electronic format all directly affect the plan.

Any changes made to the plan should be documented, including the change number, the date of the change or revision, pages of the plan affected, and a description of the change or revision. This information gives a history of plan development from its existence to the current time. The coordinator sends copies of all changes and revisions to each plan holder. Allowing a plan to exist without exercising or updating it is equivalent to having no plan.

Test the Plan

A common strategy used by many organizations is disaster simulation. During simulation, include scenarios designed to test all aspects of the plan. By doing so, appropriate response actions should be evident. Ultimately, individuals involved in the testing phase are then more knowledgeable of the procedures of other functions of the organization.

Testing or exercising an emergency response plan takes place in two stages: (1) initial testing during plan development and (2) application and periodic testing after the plan is in place. The purpose of conducting exercises is to ensure that the plan is functional and to train employees.

The purpose of testing or exercising the plan is to:[9]

- Evaluate the organization's emergency response current competence.

- Identify areas for improvement or missing information.

- Highlight assumptions that need to be questioned.

- Provide information and instill confidence in exercise participants.

- Develop teamwork.

- Raise awareness of emergency response or business continuity throughout the organization by publicizing the exercise.

- Test the effectiveness and timeliness of restoration procedures at the end of the exercise.

An organization's test program should include:[10]

- Annual testing (at a minimum) of alert, notification, and activation procedures—with recommended quarterly testing of such procedures—for continuity personnel.

- Annual testing of plans for recovering vital records (both classified and unclassified), critical information systems, services, and data.

- Annual testing of primary and back-up infrastructure systems and services (e.g., for power, water, fuel) at continuity facilities.

- Annual testing and exercising of required physical security capabilities.

- Testing and validating equipment to ensure the internal and external interoperability and viability of communications systems, through quarterly testing of the continuity communications capabilities (e.g., secure and nonsecure voice and data communications).

- Annual testing of the capabilities required to perform an organization's essential functions, as identified in the BPA.

- A process for formally documenting and reporting tests and their results.

- Annual testing of internal and external interdependencies identified in the organization's continuity plan, with respect to performance of an organization's and other organizations' essential functions.

Coordinating exercise activities requires a great deal of planning. Emergency response test exercises should be conducted at least annually. An **emergency response test exercise** is a simulated emergency event used to test the validity of an emergency plan. Plan coordinators can change the type of exercise and the scenario that they simulate each year to provide broad training. For example, one year the coordinator can plan a tabletop exercise; the following year, a functional exercise; and the third year, a full-scale exercise. The cycle begins again every three to four years.

Response teams in geographic areas prone to emergencies may want to simulate the emergency event annually, before the season starts. In Florida, for example, annual hurricane exercises should be performed in the spring. Uncommon emergencies can be simulated using the three-year cycle described previously. Overall preparation is a primary consideration, and whatever exercise frequency or schedule will ensure that organization personnel are ready to handle emergencies is the one that should be used.

QUICK TIP

Small business owners should test their emergency response plans even though the scale may be smaller than that of a large organization. If a few employees can get together to simulate an emergency and discuss their individual roles, the organization will benefit by having better informed and trained employees.

Design and Plan Test Exercise

Organizations can use several types of periodic testing. The types discussed here are defined by the U.S. Homeland Security Exercise and Evaluation Program (HSEEP) and were designed to provide common exercise policy and program guidance that constitutes a national standard for exercises.[11] **Discussion-based exercises** include *seminars, workshops, tabletop exercises,* and *games.* They highlight existing plans, policies, mutual aid agreements, and procedures, and are tools to familiarize organizations and personnel with an entity's current or expected capabilities. Discussion-based exercises typically focus on strategic, policy-oriented issues.

Seminars are informal discussions, unconstrained by real-time portrayal of events, led by a presenter, and are used to provide an overview of authorities, strategies, plans, policies, procedures, protocols, response resources, and/or concepts and ideas.

Workshops are often employed in conjunction with exercise development to determine objectives, develop scenarios, and define evaluation criteria. They differ from seminars in that participant interaction is increased, and the focus is on achieving or building a product such as a draft plan or policy.

Tabletop exercises involve key personnel discussing hypothetical scenarios in an informal setting. They can be used to assess plans, policies, and procedures or to assess types of systems needed to guide the prevention of, response to, or recovery from a defined incident.

A *game* is a simulation of operations using rules, data, and procedures designed to depict an actual or assumed real-life situation. A game typically serves three purposes: (1) to explore the processes and consequences of decision making; (2) to conduct "what if" analyses of existing plans; and (3) to develop new plans. Games use rules, data, and procedures; are designed to depict an actual or assumed real-life situation; often involve two or more teams, usually in a competitive environment; and can include models and simulations. Games do not involve the use of actual resources.

Operations-based exercises are a category of exercises characterized by actual response, mobilization of apparatus and resources, and commitment of personnel, usually held over an extended period of time. Operations-based exercises can be used to validate plans, policies, agreements, and procedures. Operations-based exercises include *drills, functional exercises,* and *full-scale exercises.*

A *drill* is a coordinated, supervised activity usually employed to test a single specific operation or function in a single organization. Drills are commonly used to provide training on new equipment, develop or test new policies or procedures, or practice and maintain current skills.

A *functional exercise* is a single or multiorganizational activity designed to evaluate capabilities and multiple functions using a simulated response. A functional exercise is typically used to evaluate the management of emergency operations centers, command posts, and headquarters, and to assess the adequacy of response plans and resources.

A *full-scale exercise* is a multiorganizational, multijurisdictional activity involving actual deployment of resources in a coordinated response as if a real incident had occurred. A full-scale exercise tests many components of one or more capabilities within emergency response and recovery, and it is typically used to assess plans, procedures, and coordinated responses under crisis conditions.

A team planning an exercise must determine the type of exercise that best meets the requirements of the organization. The best exercise type for a given year can be identified through:

- Analysis of the capabilities the entity is attempting to validate
- The training and exercises that the entity has already conducted
- The resources available for exercise planning, conduct, and evaluation

Conduct Pre-Exercise Briefing

Personnel involved in exercise evaluation should be fully briefed on all exercise activities and how the emergency response plan should work. Adequate time should be allowed for questions and last-minute exercise modifications.

Conduct Exercise

The lead participant or chief coordinator must ensure that all personnel know that the event is a simulation but that they should exercise according to the plan. Evaluation team members should be in place and ready to document exercise activities as they happen. An exercise evaluator should be at the primary command center to monitor the chief emergency coordinator and overall exercise activities.

Evaluate and Critique the Exercise

No matter what method of exercise the organization undertakes, participants should conduct a post-exercise critique. Critiquing the exercise is a useful tool for understanding both strengths and weaknesses of the emergency response plan. Critiques should indicate lessons learned plus the extent of the exercise activities. Surviving a disruptive event includes learning from mistakes. The most comprehensive plan will have gaps and deficiencies. After the plan has been successfully tested, incorporating needed modifications into the plan will improve its effectiveness.

"In November 1998, around 2 A.M., a tornado swept through Columbia, Missouri, in a matter of minutes. The microfilm operations department and another department, University Press, were temporarily relocated to a cold site (an alternative site requiring extensive effort to become operational) and were operational within eight days. The record center, after some temporary repairs, was able to provide limited services to customers by day three. Amazingly, no records were blown from the building or lost.

Fortunately, the records management staff had prepared a plan far in advance of the storm. Without one, they would never have been able to be up and running again so quickly."[12]

Lesson Learned
A team, with a designated chairperson, should be established to develop the emergency management plan, work with upper management, and educate employees on procedures.

CHAPTER 6 CHECKLIST

☐ Establish a planning team.

☐ Include budget considerations.

☐ Estimate costs.

☐ Determine response strategy.

☐ Determine recovery strategy.

☐ Collect data.

☐ Develop the emergency response plan.
    ☐ Policy statement
    ☐ Responsibilities and authority
    ☐ Task organization
    ☐ Information distribution procedures
    ☐ Preparedness checklist
    ☐ Response checklist
    ☐ Recovery checklist
    ☐ Training programs
    ☐ Testing procedures
    ☐ Review and update responsibilities
    ☐ Communications directory
    ☐ Continuity or succession of authority
    ☐ Damage assessment
    ☐ Financial or funding information
        ☐ Start-up costs
        ☐ Plan maintenance costs
        ☐ Contingency fund

☐ Approve the plan and train personnel.

☐ Review and update the plan.

☐ Test the plan.
    ☐ Design the type of exercise.
    ☐ Plan and develop the exercise.
    ☐ Develop an exercise package.
    ☐ Conduct a pre-exercise briefing.
    ☐ Conduct the exercise.
    ☐ Evaluate and critique the exercise.

NOTES

1. Michael Wallace and Lawrence Webber, *Disaster Recovery Handbook: A Step-by-Step Plan to Ensure Business Continuity and Protect Vital Operations, Facilities, and Assets* (AMACOM, 2004), 104.

2. *Disaster Recovery Journal – Glossary.* 26 March 2011 *<http://www.drj.com/tools/tools/glossary-2.html>*.

3. Ian Charters FBCI, *A Management Guide to Implementing Global Good Practice in Business Continuity Management, Glossary* (Business Continuity Institute, United Kingdom: 2008), 15, 18.

4. _____, *A Management Guide to Implementing Global Good Practice in Business Continuity Management, Section 3: Determining BCM Strategy* (Business Continuity Institute, United Kingdom: 2008), 5.

5. Federal Emergency Management Agency, *Emergency Management Guide for Business and Industry,* FEMA 141, October 1993, 48.

6. Federal Trade Commission, *Dealing with Data Breach.* 26 March 2011 *<http://www.ftc.gov/bcp/edu/microsites/idtheft/business/data-breach.html>*.

7. David N. Ammons, *Administrative Analysis for Local Government: Practical Application of Selected Techniques* (Athens: The University of Georgia, 1991), 58, 89.

8. United States General Accounting Office, *Disaster Assistance: Federal, State, and Local Responses to Natural Disasters Need Improvement* (Washington: GAO, 1991), 14-15.

9. Ian Charters FBCI, *A Management Guide to Implementing Global Good Practice in Business Continuity Management, Part 5: Exercising, Maintaining & Reviewing BCM Arrangements* (Business Continuity Institute, United Kingdom: 2008), 8.

10. Federal Emergency Management Agency, *Continuity Guidance Circular 1 (CGC 1): Continuity Guidance for Non-Federal Entities* (January 21, 2009), K-1.

11. U.S. Department of Homeland Security, *Homeland Security Exercise and Evaluation Program, Volume I* (2007), 10-11.

12. Willie M. Jones, "Trial by Tornado," *InfoPro,* ARMA International (March 2000): 37.

SECTION IV:
RESPONSE

Response is the activities taken immediately before, during, or directly after a disruptive event that minimize damage or improve recovery of records and information. Activating the emergency response plan and initiating contingency plan activities are the primary response activities.

Activating the Plan

"The purpose of the Emergency Operations Center is to command, and the key to commanding is communications."[1]

The response phase of emergency or business continuity management activates the emergency response plan. Response activities are activated during each of three stages:

1. Prehazard

2. Emergency: Hazard effects are ongoing

3. Emergency: Hazard effects have ceased[2]

Recognize an Emergency

The person (or chief coordinator) who has the overall responsibility for the emergency response plan will initiate plan activation when a disruptive event is imminent or when the need for response is recognized. An imminent event is recognized during the pre-hazard stage and allows some mitigation activities to be initiated. For example, a hurricane response plan can be activated well before landfall of the hurricane, or protective actions can be initiated when a tornado warning is issued. The plan can also be activated when an electronic sensing device, such as a fire or smoke alarm, is triggered and, therefore, warns of a pending event.

As soon as an event occurs and is recognized, the response plan is activated and continues in place while the hazard effects are ongoing and up to a certain point after the hazard effects have ceased. V1 and V2 priority vital records are deployed at the appropriate stage both during the event and immediately after hazard effects have ended.

Sometimes an event may occur, but the threat is not detected in time to respond. If this situation happens, the emergency may become a disaster. For example, perhaps a water pipe breaks during the weekend when no one is around to detect it. By the time that employees arrive Monday morning, a major flood has severely damaged the facility and its records and information.

The ability to recognize a disruptive event can be enhanced through education and training. Employees should be trained on what to look for, when to look, and where to look, which can help mitigate many disruptive events. For example, if employees can be trained to look for and shut off nonessential equipment before they leave work for the weekend, potential fires can be avoided. The site survey described in Chapter 3 can aid in detecting potential hazards and be used to train employees to recognize a potential event based on those findings.

> **QUICK TIP**
>
> Most likely, a small business owner will not have resources available to install all needed systems to detect events such as heat, humidity, smoke, water leaks, and chemicals. However, small business owners can concentrate on those systems that are most important for protecting their particular products or services.

Contact the Proper Authority

Once a threat is perceived, the potential emergency must be expressed to the proper authority. This authority is responsible for making the decision to report the event. Information needed when reporting a disruptive event consists of the following:

- Specific nature of the event

- Time of the event

- Location of the event

- Extent of damage or status of the event

- Danger or injuries to people

- Cause of the event (if known)

As mentioned in Chapter 6, the emergency response plan outlines a chain of authority, chain of command, or other reporting process to ensure accurate and timely communication. More commonly used forms of communication, such as face-to-face, telephone, cellphones, two-way radios, and pagers, are effective during an event. Fax machines, voice mail, and email are less-effective communication methods because of time delays caused by transmission and retrieval of messages, and the possibility of power loss affecting the equipment necessary to transmit and access the information.

Activate the Plan

If the designated chief coordinator is unavailable, the person who makes the initial reporting should refer to the succession-of-authority list and contact the next person in command. This person will make the initial report and activate the plan without delay. **Activation** is the result when all or a portion of a response plan is implemented or set into motion. It can also apply to portions of plan activation such as the activation of a command and control center.

> Ensuring personal safety is top priority!

If immediate danger exists for people, the first decision is determining how to protect them. In many situations, a clear and immediate decision is necessary to notify the fire department, police department, or a hazardous material response team. Coordinators may also ask the person who reported the emergency to initiate a call to a public service agency such as the fire department.

Gather and Brief the Response Team

Once the most immediate responses have been made, the emergency response team is notified and activated. The emergency response plan may identify a specific response team; however, some coordinators prefer to put a response team together based on the type of emergency. Whichever method is used, the response team must be assembled quickly.

Once the response team members have gathered, they must be briefed on the status of the emergency. Team members then review the response plan and apply documented activities to the impending event. They discuss any additional tasks that may need to be done, and specific tasks are assigned to team members.

Team members may need to decide which phase of an emergency exists. A clear delineation between the response phase and the recovery phase may not be recognizable. If the event has not yet occurred but is potentially going to occur or if the event has just begun, the team will focus on the response phase. Once the event has occurred, the team will focus on controlling the event to prevent it from becoming a disaster. If an event occurred that spontaneously resulted in a disaster, the team will focus on recovery.

Team members are also responsible for notifying others in the organization of the event. Communication should take place horizontally and vertically, top down and bottom up. Poor communication within an organization's structure will result in problems and inefficiency during a disruptive event.

Activate Emergency Command Center

An **emergency command center** is a centrally located facility that has adequate resources to maintain operations during an emergency. It is usually a temporary facility used by the response and recovery teams to coordinate the processes until alternative sites are functional. The command center must be established and readied for use, with its physical location well known to response team members, long before an event occurs. Most organizations will have a well-known control point that can serve as the command center. It will be located in a facility that has all necessary equipment and furnishings to send and receive information. The chief coordinator delegates tasks and makes decisions from the command center.

A command center should have the following resources:[3]

- The emergency communication directory
- Copies of the emergency response plan
- Records and information needed to respond to the emergency
- Reference manuals, including maps and building floor plans
- Back-up source of electricity (portable generator, etc.)
- Emergency lighting (battery-operated emergency lights, flashlights, etc.)
- Communications equipment (telephones, cellphones, ham or two-way radios, fax machines, etc.)
- Computers, laptops, and printers (with Internet access)
- Battery-operated radios (with extra batteries or battery chargers), cable television
- Message boards and presentation materials and equipment
- Office supplies
- Work area setup (desks, chairs, filing equipment, shelving, etc.)
- Personal protective equipment, including first-aid kits
- Food, water, and other personal supplies to last several days
- Sanitary facilities (internal and external)

Some essential records are created and maintained during the course of the event that should document actions taken, the timeline of the actions taken, and an account of funds spent. Names of individuals completing each action should be documented, and a roster of response team members should be maintained. These records should be included on the organization's retention and disposition schedule for accountability and retention after the event.

Other recommended documentation includes:

- Communication logs for ingoing and outgoing messages
- The physical location of the organization's vital records
- A log of injuries sustained if applicable
- Damage assessment records (generally needed for insurance purposes)
- Other records useful later in the lessons learned phase

Alternative locations should be available in the event that the primary location is involved in the emergency. A minimum of three possible emergency command centers can be identified in the response plan. The <u>first</u> location is customarily a routine emergency center, intended for contained disasters. Often operating out of an organization's security office, its location is generally, by default, known to all.

The <u>second</u> location is the facility functioning as the primary emergency command center. Intended for long-term resumption and recovery efforts, it is established to address major disasters. A back-up facility, the <u>third</u> location, is utilized only if the primary emergency command center becomes unusable.

Maintain Communications

The coordinator will want to meet with the response team often throughout the duration of the emergency. These meetings will be effective for brainstorming and solving special problems as they occur. The meetings will also provide continuity to the process by maintaining effective communication on the status of recovery efforts.

Equally important is communication with those individuals and entities outside the emergency command center. The information trail must flow from executive level management to stakeholders (employees, customers, suppliers) and news media. As the information flows, appropriate communication channels must be employed to ensure its accuracy and integrity.

Communication to organization management is used to request additional resources, equipment, and tools. Regular voice communications, such as direct or conference telephone calls, can be used. Periodic management updates can be provided via email or voicemail box. This voicemail box should be a different voicemail box than the one for all employees.

For communication to employees not present at the recovery site and their families, a voicemail box with regularly updated announcements can be effective. Be sure the telephone number is widely published before an emergency occurs.

Communication to customers is necessary to apprise them of the status of their orders. Customer good will can be maintained by calling each customer individually to assure them of shipment or to advise them of the estimated delay.

Communication to the public and news media includes letting them know what is happening with the recovery effort. Email, fax, and onsite interviews can be useful to get out the message.

Communication to the recovery team can be enhanced by using a large whiteboard with the status of the various efforts clearly printed."[4]

Initiate Recovery Activities

After the proper authority declares the event over, recovery and damage assessment activities can take place. Coordination of initial damage assessment and recovery activities will continue from the command center until the chief coordinator determines that the organization is in condition to resume normal operations.

Following an event that results in damage to an organization, the chief coordinator should initiate efforts to gather damage and emergency impact information. Damage assessment occurs in two phases:

1. The first phase is the **initial damage assessment (IDA),** a cursory review of damage caused by an emergency, disruptive event, or disaster that should be completed within the first few hours after the event has occurred.

2. The second phase is a comprehensive damage assessment, which is discussed in Section V.

IDA occurs within the first 24 hours after an event occurs. The objective is to get a good estimate of damage to report to the insurance company. In a community-wide disaster, the damage report is made to the local government emergency coordinator. The chief emergency coordinator for the organization organizes the IDA efforts.

Assemble a Damage Assessment Team

The chief coordinator assembles the IDA team. Depending on the scope of the organization, team size can range from one to several individuals. The chief coordinator gives IDA team members specific instructions on what to look for, where to look, and what to document. Finally, the chief coordinator designates a time for the team to report to the command center.

Train the Damage Assessment Team

Training is important to ensure smooth and accurate damage assessment. Gathering the information correctly and efficiently can ensure that the insurance company appropriately compensates the organization and assists in more compliant FEMA or SBA submissions for recovery funding.

Additionally, an accurate damage assessment will also ensure that the organization can obtain adequate loans to recover fully from the event.

Gather Initial Damage Estimates

The IDA team attempts to gather the initial estimates as quickly and thoroughly as possible so that recovery efforts can begin and important information is not left out of the report. IDA requires a balance between time and accuracy. The chief coordinator decides the extent of information that the team gathers and prepares a checklist for the damage assessment. The checklist may list the following items:

- Facility structural damage

- Damage to products, materials, or supplies

- Damage to records and information

- Damage to vehicles or equipment

- Damage to property

- Personal injuries

- Estimated costs to recover (materials and supplies, repairs and maintenance, and labor)

- Loss of revenue

After the team gathers the needed information, it reports to the command center. The initial damage assessment report shown in Figure 7.1 may be prepared by the IDA Team.

Compile Information Into a Report

The IDA information must then be combined into a report for the insurance company, local officials, or for organization records. Timing is very important. If the IDA information is compiled in time, it can be submitted to the insurance claims representative when he or she arrives for the inspection. IDA information can also be helpful to verify the insurance company's estimates.

The initial damage assessment is a quick financial estimate of damage. Assessments for recovery operations need to be reviewed within the first 24 hours following a disaster and are used to help specify the recovery and salvage processes that must be undertaken.

Because insurance coverage is a major factor in the recovery process, the insurance claims representative or adjuster will play a key role in assessing damage and often is included as part of the damage assessment team. During the recovery process, recovery expenses, such as repairs, travel, telephone, equipment, or facility rentals, should be tracked and documented for submittal to the insurance company.

Initiate Security Activities

Security of an organization's assets should be a high priority and must be considered in the prevention, response, and recovery phases of an emergency. Tightening security is good risk management. As discussed in Section II, adequate security measures can help prevent or greatly mitigate disruptive events. The ability to control security is important to emergency response activities. Disruptive events can divert the attention of employees and make the organization susceptible to additional damage.

Events may have residual effects—vulnerabilities or weaknesses while attempting to deal with an emergency situation. Examples include:

- A storefront window is broken during a storm. A passerby enters the store and takes thousands of dollars worth of merchandise.

- A hurricane is approaching, and residents evacuate the area. However, looters decide to stay behind and vandalize businesses while the merchants are away. They set fires to cover up the evidence.

Initial Damage Assessment Report

Facility Damaged: *Plant 1*

Location: *Adjacent to reservoir*

(Attach map with clearly marked location and travel route to site, if needed.)

Describe Damage or Injuries: *Extensive damage to plant structure and interior components. No personal injuries. Equipment water/mud damaged; records and information water/mud damaged.*

List Work Needed to Repair Damaged Site: *Water/mud up to 4' deep. Needs to be pumped out and cleaned. Equipment and components severely damaged by water/mud. Requires mechanical/electrical/structural staff. Records and information cannot be accessed until plant de-watered and determined safe.*

List Work That Has Been Completed: *None.*

(Attach activity report if any work has been completed.)

Estimated Cost: *$250,000*

(Develop a detailed breakdown of personnel, equipment, and materials for complete damage assessment; include estimate of any loss of revenue.)

Notes/Comments:

Damage Report Completed By: _____   **Date:** *3/15/11*

Initial Damage Assessment Report   Form REM2   Rev: January 3, 2011

Figure 7.1 Initial Damage Assessment (IDA) Report

- The command center is full of activity, and many people are coming and going. In all the commotion, unauthorized personnel have slipped in and stolen some confidential records.

Some practical measures can be taken to improve security. Typical security initiatives include:

- Issuing identification badges to employees and other authorized personnel
- Locking doors if personnel cannot monitor the facility during an emergency
- Installing signs designating secured or restricted areas
- Securing cash operations immediately
- Requiring sign-in at the command center and logging time in/out
- Creating a list of authorized personnel and monitoring it
- Ensuring that personnel know who is authorized to make decisions
- Maintaining supplies to board up windows quickly
- Asking police and security personnel for assistance

Recovery operations outside a facility can also be secured. Guidelines include:[5]

- Establishing rules about who is in charge
- Determining safety and operating conditions for allowing access to the area
- Distributing passes to those permitted to enter
- Setting up a security patrol or monitoring system

The proactive measure of establishing security controls in both the mitigation phase and during the response phase prevents further loss and damage during an event.

> **DISASTER SNAPSHOT**
>
> "…a six-story paper storage warehouse owned by Iron Mountain in east London caught fire and burned to the ground…BBC News said flames shot up 20 to 30 feet in the air from the building that housed 'archived, inactive business records,' according to Iron Mountain. The fire burned itself out after two days and resulted in a total loss of all the records contained inside." It was estimated that paper records of more than 600 customers were destroyed along with the building. Investigations to determine the cause of the fire included why sprinkler systems failed to work and the possibility that suspicious activity may have been a cause of the blaze. As a result, Iron Mountain reviewed its security procedures, added more security staff at its facilities, conducted additional reviews, and instigated background checks on personnel and all third parties it works with.
>
> Source: ARMA International, "Iron Mountain Facilities Burn," *The Information Management Journal*, November/December 2006: 18.

Activate Contingency Arrangements

As the response phase progresses, planned contingency arrangements need to be implemented to continue operations and business activities. These arrangements include setting up alternative operating sites, restoring V2 priority records and information for access, initiating alternative computer operations, and commencing contracts for back-up equipment.

At a minimum, vendors under contract to provide a contingency product or service should be contacted and placed on standby. This step will help assure timely delivery of the product or service. Lack of pre-signed contracts for contingency products or services can result in a product or service being unavailable or too expensive following the event, especially if the disruption is widespread. Comprehensive emergency or continuity planning includes contingency planning. **Contingency planning** is advance planning and preparedness activities undertaken with the goal of minimizing loss of vital business elements. With proper planning, an organization can quickly and effectively restore operations in the event of an emergency.

If an organization is unable to continue functioning at its normal location, an alternative site must be used to resume limited or full operations. Before full operations can resume, the organization must shut down and secure the existing facility. Employees should be prepared and trained for achieving an orderly shutdown as part of the preparation phase.

Proper planning to shut down all internal processes can yield three benefits:[6]

1. Nonessential equipment, processes, and systems are shut down

2. Essential equipment, processes, and systems remain active

3. Facility is secured from intentional damage

Some considerations to include for a planned move to an alternative facility:

- Setting up teams to focus on specific aspects of the move such as packing and moving, arranging for furnishings, coordinating equipment relocation, and maintaining security

- Documenting responsibilities and actions taken to provide an audit trail

- Arranging for an employee assistance professional to come in and talk to employees about stress, change, and personal finance

- Establishing reasonable expectations for the way personnel are to behave and perform

Security measures and contingency arrangements are strategies that help an organization respond to and recover from a disruptive event. Organizations that do contingency planning and, in particular, alternative site planning, will have a more positive experience dealing with an event.

"Having an up-to-date collection disaster plan in place facilitated the University of Hawaii at Manoa Library's successful response to a disaster caused by a flashflood. At 8:00 PM on Saturday, October 30, 2004, a flashflood carrying mud and debris hit the Library with astonishing force. A seven-foot wall of water surged through the ground floor of the Library knocking out walls. The water threw desks, shelving, filing cabinets, card files, etc., against retaining walls in the technical services area, blockading doors with towers of heavy debris. The Library's important map collection, as well as government documents, the technical services departments (cataloging, acquisitions and serials), as well as the graduate program in Library and Information Services were all located in the ground floor... The Library's Preservation Department has a collection disaster plan in place. With thorough knowledge of the collection disaster plan, a first responder's team (Library Administration, Map and Government Document Librarians, the Preservation Department) was able to make essential decisions within the first critical hours of a disaster... At dawn the next morning the staff was in place to assess the damage and to begin salvage of priority collections."

Lesson Learned

"Having a disaster plan for collections provided a core strategy that was adapted to respond to a disaster of this scale. Well-trained staff was able to organize triage and salvage priority collections."[7]

CHAPTER 7 CHECKLIST

☐ Recognize an emergency.

☐ Contact the proper authority.

☐ Activate the plan.

    ☐ Gather and brief the response team.

    ☐ Notify other personnel.

    ☐ Activate emergency command center.

    ☐ Maintain communications.

    ☐ Initiate recovery activities.

    ☐ Assemble a damage assessment team.

    ☐ Train the damage assessment team.

    ☐ Gather initial damage estimates.

    ☐ Compile information into a report.

☐ Initiate security activities.

☐ Activate contingency arrangements.

NOTES

1. Michael Wallace and Lawrence Webber, *Disaster Recovery Handbook: A Step-by-Step Plan to Ensure Business Continuity and Protect Vital Operations, Facilities and Assets* (New York: AMACOM, 2004), 104.

2. Jeffrey B. Bumgarner, *Emergency Management* (California: ABC CLIO, Inc., 2008), 28

3. Robert B. Kelly, *Industrial Emergency Preparedness* (New York: Van Nostrand Reinhold, 1989), 59.

4. Wallace and Webber, *Disaster Recovery Handbook,* 102.

5. Ronald W. Perry, "Managing Disaster Response Operations," chapter in *Emergency Management: Principles and Practice for Local Government* (Washington, DC: International City Management Association, 1991), 221-222.

6. Kelly, *Industrial Emergency Preparedness,* 62.

7. Lynn Ann Davis, "Disaster October 2004: Lessons Learned from Flashflood at University of Hawaii at Manoa Library (Honolulu, Hawaii)" World Library and Information Congress: 72d IFLA General Conference and Council, 20-24 August 2006, Seoul, South Korea, 2.

SECTION V:
RECOVERY

Recovery is the implementation of short-term activities that restore vital records and information to minimal operating standards. Disruptive event recovery for records and information includes five steps: (1) damage assessment, (2) stabilization, (3) salvage, (4) restoration, and (5) resumption of operations. The degree of effort and complexity of tasks required to achieve full recovery depends on the type of event, the amount of damage, and the effectiveness of the emergency response plan.

Recovery and Resumption of Operations

"For all damaged or destroyed property a company must understand when they need to try to restore the property, and when it can just be replaced."[1]

The *recovery phase* includes short-term activities that restore critical records and information to minimal operating standards. Recovery activities are intended to restore the organization to an acceptable condition as close as possible to that which existed prior to the event. Recovery from a disruptive event for records and information can be as simple as responding to the loss of data due to an equipment malfunction or as complex as records salvage following a hurricane. For community-wide disasters, no recovery procedures can begin until the disruptive situation has stabilized. Earthquakes, tornadoes, and hurricanes destroy much of a community's infrastructure—roads, telephone service, water distribution systems, electric power lines, and gas lines. Some locations may be physically inaccessible for days or weeks, adding considerable time to the recovery of critical information and prolonging the exposure of records and information to damaging elements. Accurate completion of the mitigation phase for critical records and information can keep damage and loss to a minimum.

Disaster recovery for records and information involves five steps:

1. Assess damage.
2. Stabilize the situation.
3. Begin salvage operations.
4. Begin restoration procedures.
5. Resume operations.

Assess Damage

The initial damage assessment (IDA) following an emergency or disaster is usually a basic estimate of the overall damage. It is generally concentrated on major facility damage such as possible structural damage, facility loss, and blocked access. Complete records and information damage assessment cannot begin until access to records holding areas and IT equipment areas is allowed.

Cost is a big factor in damage assessments. An organization may not have the funds to attempt recovery of all records and information damaged by the disruptive event. Records and information recovery is established by the vital records program during the mitigation phase and included in the emergency response plan to speed recovery efforts. Recovery priority is given to designated vital records.

Damage assessment steps include:

1. Contact recovery service.
2. Perform initial damage assessment (IDA) for records and information.
3. Determine recovery priorities based on vital records matrix.

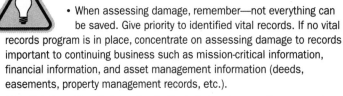

QUICK TIPS — ASSESS DAMAGE

- When assessing damage, remember—not everything can be saved. Give priority to identified vital records. If no vital records program is in place, concentrate on assessing damage to records important to continuing business such as mission-critical information, financial information, and asset management information (deeds, easements, property management records, etc.).
- Identify information that may be duplicated elsewhere such as property deeds, bank information, or tax information housed with a contracted accounting firm.
- Photograph all damage.
- Contact your contracted recovery service immediately and have a representative present when you do the damage assessment walk-through. Use a damage assessment report form so that all records are assessed consistently and you remember to record all pertinent information for every record group.
- Categorize records and information according to one of three options:
    1. Destroyed or unsalvageable records and information
    2. Unharmed, retained records and information
    3. Damaged records and information requiring recovery techniques

Concentrate limited resources on stabilizing the unharmed records and on recovering and restoring the damaged records.

Contact Recovery Service

If a records and information recovery service is under contract, the vendor must be contacted as soon as the disruptive event occurs or is noticed. In some natural disaster situations, recovery services will send recovery and response teams into the probable strike area. Recovery service representatives usually conduct some form of damage assessment on arrival and may be included on the damage assessment team if notified early enough. However, the initial assessment must take place as quickly as possible and is the responsibility of the organization. Contacting a recovery service not under contract must wait until immediately following the event, and one may not be available as soon as needed.

Perform Initial Damage Assessment (IDA) for Records and Information

Damage assessment includes several factors. Obviously, some appraisal of the physical condition of the records and information is necessary. Determine quickly whether any records or information has been completely destroyed or is inaccessible. During the September 11, 2001, attacks on the World Trade Center in New York City, many records were buried under the collapsed floors of the buildings, and others were scattered throughout nearby neighborhoods. Not only were they immediately irretrievable, but they also were never recovered before disposal of the building rubble.

Preliminary appraisal of records and information damage includes: appraising the physical condition of IT equipment and data media, appraising the physical condition of damaged records and records media, determining whether any records are completely destroyed or inaccessible, and completing the records and information damage assessment report. See a sample records and information damage assessment form in Figure 8.1.

Records and information damage assessment factors include:

- What is the extent of damage? Are areas of the facility collapsed or under water? Do records and information or computer equipment have extensive damage? Are some records and information recoverable, or is the loss total?

- What kind of damage occurred—fire, water, collapsed structure, chemical contamination, or hard drive crash?

Records and Information Damage Assessment Report

Facility: _Plant 1_

Location: _Adjacent to reservoir_

Name of person in charge at site: _Mr. E. Coordinator_   Phone/Pager: # _123-4567_

Directions to site: _____

Where and to whom to report: _Plant entrance, Mr. E. Coordinator_

Identification needed: [X] Yes   [ ] No

Type of Damage: [ ] Fire   [ ] Smoke   [X] Water   [ ] Chemical   [ ] Insect   [ ] Other

Localized: [ ] Yes   [X] No   Entire facility: [X] Yes   [ ] No

Extent of damage: [X] Heavy   [ ] Moderate   [ ] Light

Description of damage: _All rooms flooded at least 4 feet deep; standing water 2-feet deep; bottom drawers of file cabinets under_ _water; all electronic files, including diskettes, wet and muddy; all PCs water damaged_

Records and Information Damaged: _paid invoices, billing files, purchase orders_

File housing damage: [X] Yes   [ ] No   Describe: _bottom drawers waterlogged, possible rust_

Container damage: [ ] Yes   [ ] No   Describe: _____

Enclosure damage: [X] Yes   [ ] No   Describe: _file folders very wet, diskettes wet and muddy,_ _PC hard drives wet_

[X] Vital   [X] Confidential   [ ] Secure   Security Code: _____

Vital records classification: [X] V1   [X] V2   [ ] V3

Media: _paper, diskettes, PC hard drive_

Stabilization techniques necessary: _packout wet paper for vacuum drying, remove in refrigerated truck, transfer PCs to mobile_ _recovery unit, clean & dry PC hard drives, restore programs & files from back-up tapes/diskettes/CDs, dry environment, treat for_ _mold & mildew prevention, treat file cabinets with rust inhibitor_

Damage Category: [ ] Unharmed   [X] Damaged—requires recovery   [ ] Destroyed/unsalvageable

---

Recovery Recommendations:

[X] Recovery service: [ ] Internal

[ ] Recovery service pack and transport: [X] Internal pack and transport

Number of internal personnel required: _5_

Supplies needed: _Cubic-foot boxes, wax paper, plastic buckets of clean water, rubber gloves, hand truck_

Damage report completed by: _Jane Doe_   Date: _01/31/2011_

Records & Information Damage Assessment Report   Form REM3   Rev: January 4, 2010

Figure 8.1 Sample Records and Information Damage Assessment Form

- Is the damage localized, or has the entire facility or community been affected?
- What media has been damaged?
- What are the vital records classifications and recovery priorities for the damaged records and information?
- Do any records or data include confidential or personally identifiable information?
- What is the scope of damage? Has damage occurred to records housing or containers? Will help be needed to move records to a safer location for recovery? Is computer equipment damaged and inaccessible?
- Can recovery be accomplished internally, or will recovery services be required? Is recovery of records and information included in the recovery contingency contract?
- Are records damaged too extensively to be worth the cost of recovery?
- What stabilization techniques are necessary?
- Which personnel will be necessary for the recovery and restoration steps?

As the damage is assessed, document the nature and extent of the damage. Video or digital recordings or photographs of the damage are important for insurance reports and to evaluate the effectiveness of the emergency management or business continuity plan. Take necessary notes to complete any required reporting for FEMA or insurance purposes. Determine whether an alternative operating site is necessary. Classify the records and information damage into one of three categories:[2]

1. Destroyed or unsalvageable records and information
2. Unharmed, retained records and information
3. Damaged records and information requiring recovery techniques

Begin records and information recovery by restoring priority records and information. If an alternative location is used, move necessary equipment, furnishings, and supplies into a cold site; install software applications to access recovered data at a cold or hot site; and restore vital records and information.

Recovery priorities are applied to:

- Records listed on the vital records matrix
- Software applications to access recovered data
- Records used to locate records and information such as indexes, file classification lists, accession analyses, location registers, and inventories
- Items of vital or important value that:
  — Have high intrinsic value.
  — Have already developed mold.
  — Are printed on parchment, vellum, or coated paper.
  — Are printed with water-soluble inks.

Stabilize the Situation

The disaster situation must be stabilized to safeguard personnel. Begin stabilizing the situation as soon as possible. Some stabilization should take place at the same time or before the assessment step. Immediate stabilization activities include turning off gas or water leaks, turning off electricity, removing or pumping out standing water,

QUICK TIPS — STABILIZE

1. Stabilize the damaged area as quickly as possible. Reducing air temperature and humidity and increasing air circulation to the damaged area helps prevent the growth of mold and mildew. If the damaged area is too large to stabilize, remove recoverable records and information and transfer to an area that can be environmentally controlled.

2. Place water-damaged microfilm and magnetic media into clean, clear water, or rinse media and place into sealed plastic bags while still wet. DO NOT ALLOW MICROFILM TO DRY before it is restored by a qualified laboratory procedure. DO NOT USE DISKETTES before they have been cleaned and inspected by qualified recovery personnel.

3. DO NOT USE HARD DRIVES before they have been professionally cleaned and restored for use by qualified recovery personnel.

4. Begin insect extermination procedures immediately on isolated infested records to prevent migration and further damage.

removing large debris that is blocking access to the records and information housing, establishing security, and reactivating alarm systems where possible.

Stabilizing the environment and removing records and data media from the situation prevent further damage to the records and information. The techniques required depend upon the nature of the event and the media involved. Some proven stabilization techniques for records and information include:

- Reduce the air temperature and humidity and increase air circulation in the damage area to prevent the growth of mold and mildew and to prevent further damage to microfilm or magnetic media.

- Remove debris where possible to prevent further crushing of records housing or magnetic or optical drives.

- Isolate items infected with mold, mildew, hazardous chemical residue, or insects. Isolate a computer hard drive that is infected with a virus to protect the rest of the electronic system.

- Place water-damaged microfilm and magnetic media in clean, clear water or rinse media and place into sealed plastic bags while still wet.

- Begin insect extermination procedures on isolated infested records immediately to prevent migration.

As the environment is stabilized, begin the removal and relocation of damaged materials. Recovery and salvage of damaged records and information usually take place at an alternative operating site or at a designated disaster recovery site. The **disaster recovery site** is the location where a disaster occurred and where site recovery and restoration actions take place. The site may be located internally or in another facility. The recovery site should be set up with adequate supplies, equipment, and furniture for salvaging the records and information.

Some organizations contract with commercial recovery services that set up and maintain recovery sites. Commercial recovery services usually establish a local recovery site for large scale disaster recovery. Small volumes of damaged records and information are usually transported to recovery service facilities. Microfilm recovery requires shipping or transporting the film to a recovery laboratory. Some information reconstruction—such as cleaning and restoring a computer hard disk—requires very specialized recovery techniques and must occur in a specialized service location.

Determine Appropriate Salvage Operations

Salvage procedures for records and information should be included in the emergency response plan. The damage assessment helps determine which recovery procedures are needed to reconstruct or restore records and information. Selected procedures must be appropriate for the type of damage—water, smoke, computer virus, or extreme heat. They must also be appropriate for the media to be salvaged—electronic, paper, microfilm, magnetic, and optical. Some salvage techniques to be aware of include:

- Vacuum drying wet paper records helps prevent the formation of mold or mildew and prevents swelling

DISASTER SNAPSHOT

Cloud Becoming a Major Disaster Recovery Strategy

Some businesses are looking at the global reach of the Internet and cloud computing as a way to extend a new form of disaster assistance—one business offering service to a company in an affected area as a way to help it keep its processes running. Cloud computing practices make the extension of this type of aid much more feasible than before.

Cloud storage company Nirvanix will shift a copy to another continent if an organization's data is in its Node 3 data center in Japan where an earthquake and devastating tsunami occurred in March 2011.

"Should our customers have the desire to move their data out of the region, we will make sure that it is transitioned smoothly and in a timely manner, with no disruption to their business operations," said Scott Genereaux, CEO of Nirvanix. The service will be provided for free, and options include moving it to a data center in New York, Los Angeles, Dallas, or Frankfurt, Germany.

Under some circumstances, virtual appliances or virtual machine images of existing workloads can be created in the enterprise data center and stored in a cloud data center. In the event of a failure of the former, the virtual machines serve as recovery mechanisms that can be reactivated in the cloud.

Source: Charles Babcock, InformationWeek, March 18, 2011. 27 March 2011 <http://www.informationweek.com/story/showArticle.jhtml?articleID=229301232>.

or warping of bound volumes. It also prevents further deterioration while recovery and restoration procedures are carried out.

- Fire-damaged records media must have soot and smoke deposits removed and odor neutralized. Charred or heat-damaged records may have to be microfilmed or photocopied to retain the information, and the originals destroyed.

- Paper records damaged by roaches and silverfish can usually be cleaned and microfilmed to salvage the information. Paper records damaged by rodents or termites are usually unsalvageable.

- Information on records damaged or affected by hazardous chemicals must usually be transferred to another media, and the original records destroyed.

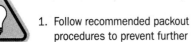

QUICK TIPS — SALVAGE

1. Follow recommended packout procedures to prevent further damage. Wet paper records must be packed in appropriate cartons, such as plastic milk crates, for drying. If using a commercial vacuum drying chamber, then clean, new cubic-foot cardboard boxes can be used. Be sure to label every box and keep an inventory of contents. Every box and crate should have a lid.

2. Handle wet paper records VERY CAREFULLY! Use plastic gloves at all times and try not to lift groups of wet records with your hands. Use a flat, straight piece of wood or plastic (such as a paint stirrer stick) to lift and separate wet paper to give more support to the length of the paper. (Also helps in spotting "critters" lodged between pages and folders.

3. Do not freeze or vacuum dry wet film (including microfilm and photos), audio- and video-tape, imaging media and magnetic media. Contact professional magnetic media recovery firms or microfilm laboratories.

Document all unsalvageable records and information as they are discarded to protect the organization in future litigation. Be sure to include all records and information known to be directly destroyed during the disaster. Be sure that records or data containing confidential or personally identifiable information are handled appropriately.

Three recovery actions are associated with the recovery of water-damaged records and information. These actions—packout, restoration, and relocation—must be performed sequentially.

Packout is the procedures and techniques used to pack and remove damaged materials from a disaster site. Prior to beginning this process, a packout goal must be established. When establishing the goal, significant focus must be placed upon the desired outcome. While some records may require restoration by a commercial recovery service, the potential exists for others to be successfully salvaged onsite.

Regardless of the packout option selected, the considerations are primarily the same. The integrity of damaged records boxes must be maintained. Documentation of individual box contents, as well as the existing assigned box number identifiers, is mandatory. When using a commercial recovery service, the recovery team may still have the responsibility of packing the materials for removal. Some larger vendors offer packing as part of their recovery services.

Wet paper records must be packed into appropriate cartons for drying. If very small volumes of paper records are wet, they may be packed and removed for air-drying. Larger volumes of wet paper records require some method of vacuum drying. **Vacuum drying** is a method of drying water-soaked documents by placing them into a vacuum chamber, creating a vacuum, and introducing warm, dry air, vaporizing water at above 32° F to remove all moisture from the records. **Vacuum freeze drying** is a method of treating water-soaked documents by freezing to prevent further damage from water in its liquid state and subsequent drying under high vacuum with the controlled application of heat, usually from heating coils installed in special shelving. The water, in the form of ice, sublimates directly from a solid state to a gaseous state.

Wet paper records require careful handling, or they can be further damaged. Records and bound volumes should be separated by wax paper or cardboard when boxed to prevent items from sticking together. File folders and bound volumes should be boxed spine down to prevent further buckling or tearing of the paper.

Use cubic-foot size boxes with cut-out handles or plastic milk cartons for easier handling. Paper should not be packed too tightly into the boxes or cartons. For successful vacuum drying, pack materials by size, with bound volumes and file folders standing upright. Label every box or carton, and make sure that every box has a lid. If file drawers are easy to remove, do not empty them; they can be dried intact.

Wet photographs, microfilm, audiotape, videotape, imaging media, and magnetic media should not be vacuum or freeze dried. Water-damaged microfilm and magnetic tape must be placed into fresh, clean water, or rinsed in clear water, placed into sealed plastic bags while still wet, and kept in a cool temperature until restored. Wet microfilm must be transported to the recovery lab within 48 hours. Magnetic tapes must be cleaned within two weeks and must not be dried with heat. Magnetic media, other than tapes, exposed to dirty, contaminated or salt water must be rinsed in clean, fresh water and allowed to air dry or be gently dried with a lint-free cloth.

Water-damaged electronic hardware, such as hard drives and PC towers, must not be turned on until they have been completely dried and inspected for corrosion potential. This inspection should be conducted by qualified professionals. Magnetic media must not be used until they have been examined for damage to the oxide layer and the data have been transferred onto other media. Recovery of electronic data can have a 95 to 100 percent success rate if immediate corrective action is taken.

Charred or soot-damaged records media must also be carefully handled. Charred paper is especially brittle and can deteriorate with rough handling. Fire-damaged media other than paper is generally packed and transported to specialized recovery services. Insect damaged records must be thoroughly fumigated before attempting to salvage the information.

Records and information damaged or contaminated by hazardous chemicals must not be handled by untrained personnel. This type of recovery or restoration requires specialized handling and removal techniques best performed by commercial recovery services

Begin Restoration Procedures

As records and information are recovered, clean, accessible facilities and housing must be available. If severe structural damage occurred, then alternative operating sites must be ready for use. Damaged file housing, retrieval equipment, and computers must be repaired or replaced. Many disaster recovery services provide location restoration as part of their contract.

HVAC systems, floors, walls, ceilings, carpets, furniture, equipment, draperies or blinds, and records housing must be thoroughly cleaned and disinfected. All traces of moisture, soot, smoke damage, chemical residue, and odor must be removed. Alternative sites must be supplied with adequate furniture and equipment, and replacement computers must be capable of supporting the existing electronic system requirements.

Restoring the work area may also include relabeling new file folders, microfilm cartridges, or CDs and DVDs. Electronic imaging media or microfilm may have to be duplicated or reformatted. Paper records may have to be resorted and placed into correct filing order. Electronic data and information will need to be restored from back-up files. Restoration priorities must be set as part of the emergency response process so that data is brought back in the correct sequence to maintain data integrity, especially in large systems. In some cases, operating systems and system configuration must be reestablished in order to restore the electronic system to full operation.

QUICK TIPS — HOUSING STAFF OFFSITE DURING A RECOVERY EFFORT

A comprehensive business continuity plan should include well-prepared steps to follow to move supplies and staff when relocating to an offsite facility following a disastrous event. Putting a plan into place well ahead of time helps create a smooth workforce transition to the alternative site.

Following a major disaster, the recovery process could take months, and staff may have to be housed for extended periods of time at the alternative location. In a regional disaster, housing choices can be extremely limited. Consider several criteria before deciding on staff housing options:

- Employees may need to bring family with them for long-term assignments.
- Employees may also need to bring family in a regional disaster where employee residences are destroyed or damaged. Roomier accommodations, as well as adequate cooking facilities, will be required.
- Employees who will be staying for extended periods will fare better in suite-type options that offer separate spaces for sleeping, relaxing, working, and eating, even without family onsite. Investigate the options near alternative sites to determine which offer the best facilities and price for extended stays. Many housing providers will work with companies to offer competitive rates for longer stays."

Source: DRJ's Information Update for Thursday, October 8, 2009, Disaster Recovery Journal, email newsletter.

Resume Operations

Relocation of the records and information to normal operational facilities takes place after the crisis has been stabilized and recovery procedures are completed. Activities to return operations to normal include:

- Cleaning and repairing or replacing the facility, furniture, and equipment.

- Restarting nonessential equipment, processes, and systems.

- Restoring nonvital records and information.

- Resorting, organizing, and indexing salvaged records and information.

- Reshelving or refiling salvaged records and information.

Environmental stabilization must be completed before moving back into the facility. Water, smoke, and insect damage must be repaired, carpeting replaced, structural damage repaired, and the environment returned to normal. Furniture, including file housing and equipment, must be repaired or replaced before records and information can be restored to the files. Nonessential equipment, processes, and systems that were shutdown prior to or during the emergency situation can be restarted as needed.

Records and information must be placed into retrievable order with current indexing before reshelving or refiling. Using photos and video or digital recordings taken during the damage assessment stage can aid in restoring records and information to predisaster order and location.

Resumption activities begin while the organization is still operating from the alternative site, which is considered a temporary location. As soon as the facility environment is stabilized and repaired, operations can be moved back into the facility. In the case of total facility destruction, the alternative site is used only until a new location is established.

Implementation actions associated with return to normal operations include:[3]

- Informing all personnel that the actual emergency, or the threat of an emergency, no longer exists, and instructing personnel on how to resume normal operations.

- Supervising either an orderly return to the normal operating facility, a move to another temporary facility, or a move to a new permanent operating facility.

- Verifying that all systems, communications, and other required capabilities are available and operational and that the organization is fully capable of accomplishing all essential functions and operations at the new or restored facility.

- Conducting an after-action review of the effectiveness of the response and recovery plans and procedures, identifying areas for improvement from the review, documenting these procedures in the organization's emergency management or business continuity plan, and then developing a remedial action plan as soon as possible after the reconstitution.

- Identifying which (if any) records were affected by the incident, and working with the records office (or similar function in the organization) to ensure an effective transition or recovery of vital records and databases and other records that had not been designated as vital records, as part of the overall reconstitution effort.

Review Lessons Learned

As normality returns to the organization, the response and recovery activities need to be evaluated. Comparing the plan to the reality of the response and recovery process aids in closing loopholes and preventing the same mistakes in the future. The review procedure should include a follow-up with all personnel involved in the response and recovery operations. Specific details and problems encountered during each step should be evaluated and appropriate changes made to the plan.

Additional training for response team members should be provided where necessary. Response and recovery supplies should be inventoried and immediately replaced. Performance of suppliers and recovery services should be evaluated and specifications updated where needed. Vendors that performed poorly may need to be replaced. Affected records and information and restored areas must be monitored regularly for any sign of continuing problems, and steps must be taken immediately to prevent further spread of the damage.

Continuity Governance

Once established, emergency and business continuity plans must be reviewed periodically and updated and revised as necessary. Audits of the plans are necessary regardless of whether the plans have been invoked during the preceding year. Organizational, legislative, and best practice changes can affect the four phases of the program and the success of the plans themselves.

Three audit methods can be used to review the programs: (1) An *external audit by a contractor or consultant* must be arranged in advance, and the vendor must have access to all emergency or business continuity management planning documentation and results of previous events requiring activation of the plans. (2) An *internal audit team* should include emergency or business continuity management professionals or other subject matter experts within the organization. Like external audits, internal audit teams must have access to all emergency or business continuity management planning documentation and results of previous events requiring activation of the plans. (3) *Self-assessments* can include reviews of a completed activation of the plans, annual risk management processes, and lessons learned.

The audit process ensures that an organization has an effective emergency management or business continuity program. The audit process has five key functions:[4]

1. To validate compliance with the organization's emergency or business continuity management policies and standards.

2. To review the organization's emergency or business continuity management solutions.

3. To validate the organization's emergency or business continuity management policies and procedures.

4. To verify that appropriate exercising and maintenance activities are taking place.

5. To highlight deficiencies and issues and ensure their resolution.

The audit recommendations and findings should be reported to organization management and should be implemented as part of the emergency or business continuity management program as soon as possible to ensure a successful response to a future disruptive event. The audit's final report should document everything done since the initiation of the audit, what improvements have been realized, and what actions remain to be implemented. The report should summarize the productivity of the entire audit process relative to the unit involved and should detail any long-term recommendations needed, including when a subsequent audit might be appropriate.[5]

Mud-covered documents, products of a flashflood, were in immediate danger of susceptibility to mold. "Four 40-foot and one 20-foot freezer shipping containers were loaded with priority materials from a staging area near the Library building exit closest to the map collection. The maps were removed in their metal drawers and carried outside. The force of the water pushed mud and debris into the map drawers. The rare maps were protected by folders, and the drawers were rinsed in the staging area to remove some of the mud prior to freezing. All of the priority maps and aerial photographs were frozen within 78 hours, and there has been no sign of mold damage caused by the disaster. To prevent a secondary disaster from mold growth to the nearly 3,000,000 volumes above the ground floor, the Library arranged for a local company to immediately provide dehumidification using generators, and to seal off the ground floor."

Lesson Learned

"Taking action to stabilize collections (by freezing and dehumidifying the building) prevents mold growth and buys time to make treatment decisions, including selection of a document recovery contractor."[6]

CHAPTER 8 CHECKLIST

Records and Information Recovery
☐ Assess damage to records and information and document the nature and extent of damage.

☐ Stabilize the situation.

☐ Prepare and pack records for recovery.

☐ Transport records to recovery site.

☐ Begin appropriate records salvage procedures.

☐ Begin restoration procedures.

Resumption of Operations
☐ Clean and repair or replace the damaged facility.

☐ Clean and repair or replace damaged furniture and equipment.

☐ Restart nonessential equipment, processes, and systems.

☐ Restore critical records and data.

☐ Resort, organize, and index salvaged records and information.

☐ Reshelve or refile salvaged records and information.

☐ Evaluate disaster response and recovery activities and make appropriate changes to the plan.

☐ Monitor affected areas for any continuing problems.

Continuity Governance
☐ Review emergency and business continuity plans.

☐ Conduct audits.

☐ Implement recommended changes to emergency and business continuity plans.

NOTES

1. Ken Doughty, *Business Continuity Planning: Protecting Your Organization's Life* (CRC Press LLC, 2001), 171.

2. Pearl Holford, comp., *Disaster Plan for the Virginia State Library and Archives* (Richmond: Virginia State Library and Archives, 1991), 8, 9.

3. Federal Emergency Management Agency, *Continuity Guidance Circular 1 (CGC 1): Continuity Guidance for Non-Federal Entities* (January 21, 2009), M-1.

4. Ian Charters FBCI, *A Management Guide to Implementing Global Good Practice in Business Continuity Management, Part 5: Exercising, Maintaining & Reviewing BCM Arrangements* (Business Continuity Institute, United Kingdom: 2008), 4.

5. J. Edwin Dietel, J.D., "Improving Corporate Performance Through Records Audits," *The Information Management Journal,* ARMA International (April 2000): 26.

6. Lynn Ann Davis, "Disaster October 2004: Lessons Learned from Flashflood at University of Hawaii at Manoa Library (Honolulu, Hawaii)," World Library and Information Congress: 72nd IFLA General Conference and Council, 20-24 August 2006, Seoul, South Korea, 3.

Final Observations

"Only a conscious, planned effort can protect vital business information from any conceivable hazard."[1]

Emergency Management for Records and Information Programs has presented a general blueprint for developing an organization-wide records and information emergency management or business continuity program. It is intended as a universal guide to the basic concepts, systematic steps, key elements, program benefits, and practical considerations in preparing, implementing, and updating such a program. A written, approved emergency management or business continuity plan is not a substitute for the good sense, sound management, and creativity required when responding to a disruptive event.

Many elements of an emergency management or business continuity plan are already in place before the decision is made to establish a formal plan. Insurance programs, site and information security policies, vital records protection through the use of remote site storage of duplicates and back-up computer tapes, and regular equipment maintenance checks are only a few program elements that often predate the formal emergency management or business continuity process. The plan, how-ever, reviews, coordinates, improves, and supplements these existing elements so that a comprehensive, cost-effective program emerges.

A number of national and state/province resources are available to assist in planning and coordinating emergency management or business continuity plans for government agencies, local governments, private businesses, and individuals. In the U.S., FEMA has a number of helpful publica-tions and other material—ranging from planning, preparation, and recovery publications and videos to flood, hurricane, and other disaster maps that can be used in determining natural disaster risk—available on its website at *www.fema.gov*. Table 9.1 lists similar websites available in other countries:

Country Websites for National and State/Province Resources		
Canada	Public Safety Canada	<http://www.getprepared.gc.ca>
Australia	Attorney-General	<http://www.ema.gov.au>
United Kingdom		<http://www.direct.gov.uk/en/governmentcitizensandrightsindex.htm>

Table 9.1 Country Websites

This book focuses on emergency management and disastrous and disruptive events. In many organizations, data and cyber security is considered separate from emergency management; but, in reality, both require planned procedures to be in place for business continuity. The boundary between cyber security and emergency management is blurred in today's business environment. Breach of sensitive or personal data, file and website hacking, and deliberate sabotage of data by disgruntled employees can cause expensive disruption of the business processes. A comprehensive, effective emergency management or business continuity plan will include response and recovery planning for any eventuality that can damage an organization's reputation and customer good will.

An emergency management or business continuity plan for records and information works most effectively in the hands of a knowledgeable, creative, and confident records and information manager. Such a manager can exert the strong leadership needed to serve as coordinator, can quickly assume the responsibility for identifying, isolating, and managing the consequences of a disruptive event, as well as for directing reconstruction and salvage of those records and data critical to the successful resumption of business following a disruptive event.

DISASTER SNAPSHOT

A former IT director in Virginia was convicted by the FBI for deleting files at his former employer. According to the Department of Justice, the IT director from Richmond, Virginia, "pleaded guilty to one count of intentionally damaging a protected computer without authorization." He was sentenced to 27 months in jail and ordered to pay $6,700 in restitution to his former employer, Transmarx, which sells telecommunications equipment and supplies. Transmarx fired the director, who had access to the company's website, in June 2008. According to court documents, "the director admitted that on July 25, 2008, he used a personal computer and an administrator account and password to access the computer hosting the Transmarx website." After accessing the computer, he knowingly caused the transmission of a series of commands that intentionally caused damage without authorization to the computer by deleting approximately 1,000 files related to the Transmark website. In pleading guilty, he admitted that he caused the damage because he was "angry about being fired."

The case is one of a string of attacks involving malicious or misguided insiders. In October 2010, for example, the FBI charged a former corporate insider with offering to supply company secrets to an unnamed foreign government. Also in October 2010, a federal jury found a contract Unix engineer for Fannie Mae guilty of having planted a malicious script designed to delete everything on the mortgage-purchasing association's networks.

While external attackers may get the limelight, malicious insiders remain a potent threat. Indeed, according to a 2010 CyberSecurity Watch Survey, 67 percent of organizations surveyed said that insider breaches resulted in greater financial losses than attacks by outsiders.

Source: Mathew J. Schwartz, "Former IT Director Imprisoned for Hacking Employer's Servers," *InformationWeek,* November 3, 2010, 02:22 PM. 19 March 2011 *<http://www.informationweek.com/news/security/attacks/showArticle.jhtml?articleID= 228200057&cid=RSSfeed_IWK_All>.*

A motion picture production and distribution company located in Southern California experienced a computer-related disaster.

"The firm employs approximately 300 full-time staff and roughly 200 contractors… The facility also houses the two small computer rooms from which all company IT Services are provided.

One day in late 2006 at around 5:00 A.M., all power to the building and the surrounding four-block area stopped. Utility crews found the source of the problem to be a rat that had chewed through high voltage cables coming out of a distribution transformer. Some residents and office workers were inconvenienced for up to eight hours."

Lesson Learned

"The following were among some of the key lessons learned from this event.

1. *Assess your threats and vulnerabilities on a regular basis.* This company had never conducted a risk assessment. This event pointed out clearly the necessity and value of doing such an assessment.

2. *Prioritize your business processes in terms of time-dependent impact.* Not all business processes have the same degree of urgency in terms of how quickly they need to be restored. Even a mini-BIA can help prioritize the sequence of restoration of business processes.

3. *Identify mitigation plans to minimize impacts in the short term.* The company discovered through its risk assessment that it had several exposures and single-points-of-failure. As a result, several mitigation plans were proposed and implemented.

4. *Propose long-term strategies to permanently reduce or eliminate risk.* While mitigation plans were intended to address the current environment, long-term strategies were proposed to permanently eliminate many of these exposures.

5. *Ensure [that] executive management is fully behind these efforts.* None of the above activities could have been successfully implemented without the full support of senior management. Ensuring [that] you have executive support is a primary requirement to ensure [that] any efforts in risk assessments, business continuity, and disaster recovery are effective."[2]

NOTES

1. Karen L. Simpson, *Value-Added Records Management: Protecting Corporate Assets and Reducing Business Risks* (New York: Quorum Books, 1992), 143.

2. Rich Schiesser, "Case Study: Recovery Reactions to a Renegade Rodent," *IT Management Reference Guide,* May 11, 2007, Update, 184.

Glossary

A – B

activation. The result when all or a portion of a response plan is implemented or set into motion. It can also apply to portions of plan activation such as the activation of a command and control center.

air-drying. A records and information recovery process that uses air as a means to remove humidity, dampness, or wetness from media.

alternative data sources. Repositories used to house replicated data and information. They can include managed service providers or network storage environment duplication.

alternative operating site. A secondary location or facility used to conduct critical business operations in the event of a disruptive event. Alternative sites can also include nontraditional options such as working from home (telecommuting) and mobile-office concepts.

ARMA International. An international professional association that is the authority on managing paper and electronic records and information.

business continuity management (BCM). A holistic management process that identifies potential impacts that threaten an organization and provides a framework for building resilience with the capability for an effective response that safeguards the interests of its key stakeholders, reputation, brand, and value creating activities.

business continuity plan (BCP). The documentation of a predetermined set of instructions or procedures that describe how an organization's business functions will be sustained during and after a significant disruption. *[NIST 800-34]*

business impact analysis (BIA). The process of looking at critical processes and determining the impact on the organization if the process is interrupted. The BIA is used to identify critical business functions and their supporting records and information, and to determine maximum acceptable loss beyond which the negative impact would be too great.

business process. A series of steps designed to produce a product or service.

business process management (BPM). The achievement of an organization's objectives through the improvement, management, and control of essential business processes.

business resumption planning (BRP). The process of planning and preparing with the goal of minimizing loss in the event of a disaster. The organization's vital functions are identified, and measures are taken to ensure that functions can be quickly and effectively restored.

C – D

classification system. A system in which related material is filed under a major subject and its subheadings. *[ARMA International, Glossary of Records and Information Management Terms, 3d ed.]*

cold site. An alternative facility that has the necessary electrical and physical components of a computer facility but does not have computer equipment in place. *[NIST 800-34]*

community-wide events. Emergencies or disasters that result in immediate disruption of communications and emergency services, power outages, and widespread destruction.

communications failure. An unplanned interruption in communication between two points that may result from a failure of hardware, software, or telecommunications components comprising the link.

contingency planning. Advance planning and preparedness activities undertaken with the goal of minimizing loss of vital business elements. With proper planning, an organization can quickly and effectively restore operations in the event of an emergency. *(See* **Business Resumption Planning.***)*

cost-benefit analysis. The process of gathering information, analyzing the data, and subsequently documenting the results to determine costs and benefits of a program.

critical business processes. Those parts or elements of an organization that are vital to everyday operations. If these critical processes are not performed, the organization may lose revenue and profits, experience increased operating costs following recovery, and possibly lose customers.

damage assessment. A process that includes assigning a team to assess the damage immediately following a disaster, documenting damage to organizational assets, and reporting the findings to the proper authority.

data replication. The process of replicating data between two or more sites to be used in the event that the primary site is unavailable.

data warehouse. A central repository for all or selected data created, used, and often maintained by the organization.

decryption. The process of converting encrypted data back into its original form using a pre-determined decryption key based on an algorithm.

designed dispersal. A duplicate records dispersal procedure established specifically to protect vital information.

disaster. An emergency event that progresses from the realm of standard operating procedures and moves to conditions requiring resources beyond the organization's means.

disaster recovery site. Location where a disaster occurred and site recovery and restoration actions take place.

disaster response site. Location where coordination of emergency support information and resources (on-scene operations) activities take place.

discussion-based exercises. Tools to familiarize organizations and personnel with an entity's current or expected capabilities that focus on strategic, policy-oriented issues. They highlight existing plans, policies, mutual aid agreements, and procedures. Discussion-based exercises include seminars, workshops, tabletop exercises, and games.

dispersal. The routine or designed transfer of duplicate records to locations beyond those where the originals are housed. *[ANSI/ARMA 5-2010]*

E – L

electronic protective storage. The process of transmitting original electronic data and/or files not contained on tape, optical disk, or other magnetic or optical physical media to offsite electronic storage.

electronic vaulting. The transfer of data to an alternative server for storage in a data warehouse or electronic vault.

emergency. A sudden, urgent, usually unexpected occurrence or occasion requiring immediate action.

emergency command center. A centrally located facility that has adequate resources to maintain operations during an emergency. Typically, it is a temporary facility used by the response and recovery team(s) to coordinate the processes until alternative sites are functional.

emergency management. A planned approach for the prevention of disasters, preparedness and response to emergencies, and recovery following an emergency or disaster.

emergency response plan. A documented plan addressing the immediate reaction and response to an emergency situation. *[Disaster Recovery Journal Glossary]*

emergency response test exercise. A simulated emergency event used to test the validity of an emergency plan. Based on the extent of the exercise, some or all elements of a plan can be tested for many different types of emergencies. Information gathered from the exercise is used to refine and improve the plan.

encryption. The conversion of data into cipher text meeting national and international standards that cannot be easily understood by unauthorized users or viewers.

hot site. A fully operational offsite data processing facility equipped with hardware and system software to be used in the event of a disaster. *[NIST 800-34]*

important records. Records and information for which a reproduction, although acceptable as a substitute for the original, could be obtained only at considerable expense and labor or only after considerable delay. *[NFPA 232-2007]*

initial damage assessment (IDA). A cursory review of damage caused by an emergency, disruptive event, or disaster that should be completed within the first few hours after the event has occurred. This information is collected by the local department of emergency management and forwarded to state and federal authorities.

localized events. Events that may include loss of life, power outages, and massive destruction; but communications and emergency services may not be affected. Localized events include tornados, localized flood, or a bombing incident.

loss prevention plan. A written, approved, implemented, and periodically tested program specifically outlining all actions to be taken to reduce the risk of avoidable disaster and to minimize the loss if a disruptive event occurs.

M – N

magnetic media. Any storage medium in which different patterns of magnetization are used to represent stored bits or bytes of information. *[ARMA International, Glossary of Records and Information Management Terms, 3d ed.]*

managed service provider. A contract service offering remote data protection services, including continuous online data backup, recovery, and electronic vaulting.

maximum tolerable period of disruption (MTPD). The timeframe during which a recovery must become effective before an outage compromises the ability of an organization to achieve its business objectives and/or survival. *[Business Continuity Institute]*

microfilm. 1. A high-resolution film in roll form containing microimages. 2. To record microimages on film. *[ARMA International, Glossary of Records and Information Management Terms, 3d ed.]*

mirroring. A method of data replication that maintains an exact copy of electronic records by applying changes at the secondary site in lockstep with or synchronous to changes at the primary site. *[ANSI/ARMA 5-2010]*

mitigation. The activities or measures taken to eliminate or reduce the probability of loss if a disruptive event occurs.

natural disaster. An event of great loss of life and property caused by natural means or the forces of nature. Categorized as geological (earthquakes), meteorological (hurricanes, tornadoes), hydrological (floods), and biological (disease pandemics).

network-attached storage (NAS). Hard disk storage set up with its own network IP address on the organization's local area network (LAN) rather than being attached to the department server used for daily work applications.

nonessential records. Records and information on a variety of media considered to be of little value to an organization. These records are usually for convenience only and not vital to the operations or existence of the organization. Examples include: routine telephone messages, employee bulletins, reading files, and various announcements.

O – P

operations-based exercises. Exercises characterized by actual response, mobilization of apparatus and resources, and commitment of personnel, usually held over an extended period of time. They can be used to validate plans, policies, agreements, and procedures. Operations-based exercises include drills, functional exercises, and full-scale exercises.

organizational events. Emergencies or disasters that are limited to a single building, floor, or office. Because of the narrow scope of these events, greater use of community and organization resources is possible.

packout. The procedures and techniques used to pack and remove damaged materials from the disaster site.

payback. That point in time when an organization's investment, or cash outlay, is returned in the form of a benefit. Emergency management requires an initial outlay of funding and investment into ensuring that the organization is prepared for a disruptive event. That return on investment is not realized until an event occurs and the actions are taken as a result of the initial funding that enabled the organization to mitigate loss.

plan maintenance costs. Those costs associated with a program that accrue after the program has been implemented. Costs that are reoccurring.

preparedness. Activities established to assist in responding to a disruptive event.

protective storage. The use of fire-resistant and environmentally-controlled records protection equipment and vaults designed for the protection of the media being stored. *[ANSI/ARMA 5-2010]*

R – S

record. Recorded information, regardless of medium or characteristics, made or received by an organization in pursuance of legal obligations or in the transaction of business. *[ARMA International, Glossary of Records and Information Management Terms, 3d ed.]*

records protection equipment. Self-contained, movable devices of varying configurations, including insulated bodies with insulated doors or drawers or lids, nonrated multidrawer devices housing individually-rated drawer bodies, and other similar constructions. The equipment must be listed or labeled protection equipment in accordance with NFPA 232. *[NFPA 232-2007]*

recovery. Activities associated with restoring resources or operations following a disruptive event.

recovery time objective (RTO). The time by which mission-critical activities and/or their dependencies must be recovered. *[Business Continuity Institute]*

response. Activities established to react immediately to an emergency event.

resumption of operations. The point of recovery when an organization begins to resume normal operations following a disruptive event.

risk. The exposure to the chance of injury or loss. *[Dictionary.com Unabridged]*

risk analysis. The process of identifying the probabilities of risk of loss or damage to records and information. (future)

risk assessment. The process of identifying existing risk to records and information. (current)

risk management. The culture, processes, and structures put into place to effectively manage potential negative events. As eliminating all risk is not possible or desirable, the objective of risk management is to reduce risks to an acceptable level. *[Disaster Recovery Journal Glossary]*

risk register. A table used to document risk information associated with an ongoing project.

risk tolerance level. The maximum exposure to risk, whether for a given type of risk or across all exposures, that is acceptable based on the benefits and costs involved. *[Lemieux, Managing Risk for Records and Information]*

routine dispersal. Dispersal of duplicate records as part of normal business practice.

shadowing. A method of data replication that maintains an exact copy of electronic records, typically by continuously capturing changes and applying them at the recovery site. *[ANSI/ARMA 5-2010]*

site survey. A review of a facility or location in which hazards or vulnerabilities, such as leaky roofs, fire hazards, lack of fire suppression, and insect infestation, are documented. A site survey can be conducted for risk assessment, damage assessment, or other purposes.

social disasters. Deliberate destructive activities causing illness, injury, and death. Examples include theft, espionage, vandalism, riots, terrorism, and war.

standard records vaults. Completely fire-resistive enclosures used exclusively for records storage. They are equipped, maintained, and supervised to minimize the possibility of origin of fire within and to prevent entrance of fire from outside for a specified period of time. The vault must be constructed according to specified ratings. *[NFPA 232-2007]*

start-up costs. Costs associated with the beginning or implementation of a new program. These costs are usually one-time costs, or initial costs to get a new program started.

storage area network (SAN). A high-speed special-purpose network that interconnects different kinds of data storage devices with associated data servers.

T – U – V

technological disasters. Events usually caused by human error or as secondary occurrences to natural disasters. Examples include the release of hazardous materials, airplane crashes, structural failures, a security breach of data, a viral attack on the computer network, and dam failures.

transaction-aware replication. A form of data replication that is typically accomplished by electronically transmitting a database or file changes (e.g., through logs) to the secondary site and applying those changes to a replicated dataset. *[ANSI/ARMA 5-2010]*

useful records. A temporary record that is normally accumulated in operations and is kept for a time period established by the organization. *[NFPA 232-2007]*

vacuum drying. The treatment of water-soaked documents by placing them into a vacuum chamber, creating a vacuum, and introducing warm dry air.

vacuum freeze drying. The treatment of water-soaked documents by freezing to prevent further damage from water in its liquid state, and subsequent drying under high vacuum with the controlled application of heat, usually from heating coils installed into special shelving. The water, in the form of ice, sublimates directly from a solid state to a gaseous state.

vital records. Records that are fundamental to the functioning of an organization. Certain vital records contain information critical to the continued operation or survival of an organization during or immediately following a crisis. Such records are necessary to continue operations without delay under abnormal conditions. They contain information necessary to recreate an organization's legal and financial status and to preserve the rights and obligations of stakeholders, including employees, customers, investors, and citizens. Some vital records may be unique and not easily reproducible, or the cost of reproduction or replacement may be considerable. They may be required in their original form to meet or fulfill evidential requirements. The term *vital records* also includes documentation subject to a vital records program such as pertinent IT systems, help manuals, or emergency contact lists. For the purposes of this book, the use of this term does *not* mean solely those birth and death records referred to as "vital records" in the vital statistics or health industry. *[ANSI/ARMA 5-2010]*

vital records matrix. A detailed list identifying the vital records, their location, protection instructions, method of protection, classification and priority, and recovery responsibility in case the records are lost during a disruptive event.

vulnerability assessment. The process of identifying, quantifying, and prioritizing (or ranking) the vulnerabilities in a system such as nuclear power plants, information technology systems, energy supply systems, water supply systems, transportation systems, and communication systems. In emergency and business continuity management, it means assessing the threats from potential hazards to the population and to the infrastructure for that particular system.

Selected Bibliography

Ammons, David N. *Administrative Analysis for Local Government: Practical Application of Selected Techniques* (Athens: The University of Georgia, 1991).

Anderson, Kayla, KOB TV. "Feds called in to help investigate downtown fire," Albuquerque, NM (Posted at: 06/25/2010 6:52 PM). 3 March 2011 <*http://www.kob.com/article/stories/S1625640.shtml?cat=504*>.

Andolsen, Alan A., CMC, CRM. "The Pillars of Vital Records Protection: Preparation & Practice," *The Information Management Journal* 42, no 2 (March/April 2008): 28-32.

Appleby, Julie. "Don't let hurricanes blow your medical records away, companies say," *USA TODAY*, Money Section, 27 October 2005, 3B.

ARMA International. ANSI/ARMA 5-2010, *Vital Records Programs: Identifying, Managing, and Recovering Business-Critical Records* (Overland Park, KS: ARMA International, 2010).

_____. "Iron Mountain Facilities Burn," *The Information Management Journal* (November/December 2006): 18.

_____. *Glossary of Records and Information Management Terms*, 3rd ed. (Lenexa, KS: ARMA International, 2007).

Ballman, Janette. "Then and Now! Small Businesses Are Finding It Difficult to Recover," *Disaster Recovery Journal* 7, no. 2 (April/May/June 1994): 34.

Bumgarner, Jeffrey B. *Emergency Management* (Santa Barbara, CA: ABC CLIO, Inc., 2008).

Bridgeman, Carleen. "Foolproof Solutions for the Foolhardy," *Disaster Recovery Journal* 7, no. 2 (April/May/June 1994): 77.

Carmichael, David W. "Lessons That Katrina Taught Me," Item 3, Meeting with Georgia Municipal and Court Associations, November 2005.

Chandler, Krishna. "Disaster Recovery – Lessons Learned from the Hurricanes," *EMS Newsletter* (October 18, 2005).

Charters, Ian, FBCI. *A Management Guide to Implementing Global Good Practice in Business Continuity Management, Section 1: BCM Policy & Programme Management* (Business Continuity Institute, United Kingdom: 2008).

_____. *A Management Guide to Implementing Global Good Practice in Business Continuity Management, Section 3: Determining BCM Strategy* (Business Continuity Institute, United Kingdom: 2008).

_____. *A Management Guide to Implementing Global Good Practice in Business Continuity Management, Part 5: Exercising, Maintaining & Reviewing BCM Arrangements* (Business Continuity Institute, United Kingdom: 2008).

_____. *A Management Guide to Implementing Global Good Practice in Business Continuity Management, Glossary* (Business Continuity Institute, United Kingdom: 2008).

Cronin, Kevin P. "Legal Necessity," *Disaster Recovery Journal* 6, no. 2 (April/May/June 1993): 26-28.

Crouhy, Michel, Dan Galai, and Robert Market, *Risk Management* (New York: McGraw-Hill, 2001).

Davis, Lynn Ann. "Disaster October 2004: Lessons Learned from Flashflood at University of Hawaii at Manoa Library (Honolulu, Hawaii)," World Library and Information Congress: 72nd IFLA General Conference and Council, 20-24 August 2006, Seoul, South Korea.

Deutsch, Dennis S. "Simple Yet Savvy," *Computerworld* 28, no. 40 (October 3, 1994): 121.

Dickstein, Dennis I., and Robert H. Flast. *No Excuses: A Business Process Approach to Managing Operational Risk* (Hoboken, NJ: John Wiley & Sons, Inc., 2009).

Dietel, J. Edwin, J.D. "Improving Corporate Performance Through Records Audits," *The Information Management Journal*, ARMA International (April 2000): 18-26.

Disaster Recovery Journal – Glossary. 3 March 2011 <*http://www.drj.com/tools/tools/glossary-2.html*>.

Doughty, Ken. *Business Continuity Planning: Protect Your Organization's Life* (CRC Press LLC , 2001).

Factory Mutual Engineering & Research. "Taking Steps to Decrease the Risk of Office Fire Losses," *Disaster Recovery Journal* 5, no. 2 (April/May/June 1992): 8-12.

Factory Mutual Systems. "Some Common Fire Causes," *Fire Safety Fundamentals,* vol. 3 (n.p., n.d.).

Ferraro, Cathleen. "Avoiding Data Disaster: Many small businesses fail to protect their core documents from the threat of calamity," *The Sacramento Bee* 4 June 2003.

Gutierrez, Crystal, KRQE TV. "100K medical records destroyed in fire. Warehouse held pre-2005 UNM Hospital files," Albuquerque, NM (Updated: Thursday, 12 Aug 2010, 7:51 PM MDT; Published: Thursday, 12 Aug 2010, 6:33 PM MDT). 4 March 2011 <*http://www.krqe.com/dpp/news/business/90%25-of-hospital-records-destroyed*>.

Holford, Pearl, comp. *Disaster Plan for the Virginia State Library and Archives* (Richmond: Virginia State Library and Archives, 1991).

Hurd, Joanne E. "Do You Know Where the Briefcase is?" *Journal of Systems Management 3X/400* 45, no. 8 (August 1994): 16-21.

Jeston, John, and Johan Nelis. *Business Process Management, Practical Guidelines to Successful Implementations* (Oxford, U.K.: Elsevier, 2006).

Jones, Willie M. "Trial by Tornado," *InfoPro,* ARMA International (March 2000): 37.

Kelly, Robert B. *Industrial Emergency Preparedness* (New York: Van Nostrand Reinhold, 1989).

KOAT TV. "National Team To Help Investigate Fire Documents Still Smoldering From Wednesday's Warehouse Fire," Albuquerque, NM (Posted: 4:02 PM MDT June 25, 2010; Updated: 5:45 PM MDT June 25, 2010). 4 March 2011 <*http://www.koat.com/r/24046306/detail.html*>.

Lee, Thomas F. "Master the Disaster!" *Office Systems95* 12, no. 4 (April 1995): 14-25.

Lemieux, Victoria L. *Managing Risk for Records and Information* (ARMA International, 2004).

McLoughlin, David. "A Framework for Integrated Emergency Management," *Public Administration Review* 45, special issue (January 1985): 165-172.

Myers, Kenneth N. *Business Continuity Strategies: Protecting Against Unplanned Disasters* (Hoboken, NJ: John Wiley & Sons, Inc., 2006).

National Fire Protection Association, Inc. *NFPA 232, Standard for the Protection of Records, 2000 Edition* (Quincy, MA: National Fire Protection Association, Inc., 2000).

National Institute of Standards and Technology, SP800-34, *Contingency Planning Guide for Information Technology Systems,* Washington, D.C. (June 2002).

Noakes-Fry, Kristen, and Trude Diamond. *Business Continuity and Disaster Recovery Planning and Management: Technology Overview* (Gartner, Inc., 11 July 2003).

Robek, Mary F., Gerald F. Brown, and David O. Stephens. *Information and Records Management: Document-Based Information Systems,* 4th ed. (New York: Glencoe, 1995).

Romero, David, KRQE TV. "Cause of 3-alarm warehouse fire unknown," Albuquerque, NM (Published: Wednesday, 23 Jun 2010, 8:47 PM MDT; Updated Thursday 24 Jun 2010, 6:34 PM MDT). 4 March 2011 *<http://www.krqe.com/dpp/news/crime/two-alarm-fire-rakes-downtown-warehouse>.*

Rummler, Geary A., and Alan P. Brache. *Improving Performance: How to manage the white space on the organizational chart* (San Francisco: Jossey-Bass, 1995).

Schmitz, Tony. "BCP vs. the Volcano," *Continuity Insights,* Volume 8, no, 3, (May/June 2010): 30-31.

Schwartz, Mathew J. "Former IT Director Imprisoned for Hacking Employer's Servers," *Information Week,* 3 November 2010, 02:22 PM. 4 March 2011 *<http://www.informationweek.com/news/security/attacks/showArticle.jhtml?articleID=228200057&cid=RSSfeed_IWK_All>.*

Springer, Joie. "UNESCO provides assistance in preserving Haitian documentary heritage," UNESCO.org. 4 March 2011 *<http://portal.unesco.org/ci/en/ev.php-URL_ID=29582&URL_DO=DO_TOPIC&URL_SECTION=201.html, 01-03-2010>.*

The Local. "Construction worker confesses in Cologne archive collapse case," *The Local: Germany's news in English* (Published: 9 Feb 10 09:08 CET). 4 March 2011 *<http://www.thelocal.de/article.php?ID=25131>.*

Towler, Grayson. "A Survivor's Tale: The Rebirth of the Federal Employees Credit Union in Oklahoma City," *Disaster Recovery Journal* 8, no. 3 (July/August/September 1995): 11-14.

United Business Media Limited. *InformationWeek* Research Brief, *Business Continuity: In the Aftermath* (London: United Business Media Limited, 2001).

United States Department of Homeland Security. *Homeland Security Exercise and Evaluation Program,* Volume I (Washington, D.C., 2007).

United States Federal Emergency Management Agency (FEMA). "Good Record Keeping Speeds Local Disaster Recovery," FEMA media release number: 1850-004, Release Date: August 4, 2009.

_____. *Continuity Guidance Circular 1 (CGC 1): Continuity Guidance for Non-Federal Entities* (Washington, D.C.: FEMA, January 21, 2009) Appendix K.

_____. *Continuity Guidance Circular 1 (CGC 1): Continuity Guidance for Non-Federal Entities* (Washington, D.C.: FEMA, January 21, 2009) Appendix M.

_____. *Emergency Management Guide for Business and Industry,* FEMA 141 (Washington, D.C.: FEMA, October 1993).

United States Federal Trade Commission. "Dealing with Data Breach." 5 March 2011 *<http://www.ftc.gov/bcp/edu/microsites/idtheft/business/data-breach.html>.*

Upfront. "Philly Clerk Allegedly Sold City Records," *Information Management,* ARMA International (November/December 2010): 11.

Vega, Cynthia, and Brad Watson. "Flooding of Dallas records office 'catastrophic,' say officials," WFAA, Dallas, Texas (Posted June 1, 2010 at 7:31 a.m.; Updated Tuesday, June 1, at 5:21 p.m. 5 March 2011 *<http://www.wfaa.com/news/local/Dallas-records-at-risk-as-water-main-break-floods-building-95307034.html >*.

Wallace, Michael, and Lawrence Webber. *The Disaster Recovery Handbook: A Step-By-Step Plan to Ensure Business Continuity and Protect Vital Operations, Facilities, and Assets* (New York: AMACOM, 2004).

Watson, Brad. "Flood at Dallas County Records Building caused $10 million in damage," WFAA, Dallas, Texas (Posted on June 8, 2010 at 2:22 p.m.; Updated Tuesday, Jun 8 at 8:13 p.m.). 5 March 2011 *<http://www.wfaa.com/news/local/Damage-to-flooded—95886509.html>*.

Wold, Geoffery H. "The Disaster Recovery Planning Process: Part I of III," *Disaster Recovery Journal* 5, no. 1 (January/February/March 1992): 29-34.

Wold, Geoffrey H., and Robert F. Shriver. "Risk Analysis Techniques," *Disaster Recovery Journal* 7, no. 3 (July/August/September 1994): 46-52.

Wolff, Richard E. "Snap, Crackle & Pop," *Records Management Quarterly* 19, no. 2, ARMA International (April 1985): 3-6.

Zimmerman, Rae. "The Relationship of Emergency Management to Governmental Policies on Man-Made Technological Disasters," *Public Administration Review* 45 (special issue January 1985): 37.

Additional Resources

The following materials are not cited in the text. They provide additional information useful for developing and implementing emergency management and business continuity plans for records and information.

ARMA International. *Evaluating and Mitigating Records and Information Risks* (Lenexa, KS: ARMA International, 2009).

Commonwealth Films. *Back in Business: Disaster Recovery/Business Resumption,* 26 min. DVD (Boston: Commonwealth Films.) 5 March 2011 *<http://www.commonwealthfilms.com>*.

_____. *Computer Virus Attack, Defending Against Viruses and Hackers,* 15 min. DVD (Boston: Commonwealth Films.) 5 March 2011 *<http://www.commonwealthfilms.com>*.

_____. *Ready For Anything, Business Continuity, Disaster Recovery, Preparedness,* 21 min. DVD (Boston: Commonwealth Films.) 5 March 2011 *<http://www.commonwealthfilms.com>*.

_____. *The Best Defense: A User's Guide to Computer Security Today,* 22 min. DVD (Boston: Commonwealth Films.) 5 March 2011 *<http://www.commonwealthfilms.com>*.

Heritage Emergency National Task Force. *Emergency Response and Salvage Wheel,* Heritage Preservation, Washington, D.C., 2005. 5 March 2011 *<http://www.heritagepreservation.org/catalog/wheel1.htm>*.

_____. *Field Guide to Emergency Response,* Heritage Preservation, Washington, D.C., 2005. 5 March 2011 *<http://www.heritagepreservation.org/catalog/product.asp?IntProdID=33>*.

International Organization for Standardization. ISO/TR 26122:2008, *Information and documentation—Work process analysis for records* (Switzerland: ISO, 2008).

Northeast Document Conservation Center. *Preservation Leaflets—Emergency Management.* 5 March 2011 *<http://www.nedcc.org/resources/leaflets.list.php>*.

Sample Forms

Purchasers of this book are entitled to download electronic versions of these forms at
www.arma.org/bookstore/materials/emergencymanagement.

Records and Information Impact and Probability Matrix				
Probability of Loss or Damage				
	Low	**Low**	**Medium**	**High**
Impact		**1** (Accept and monitor risk)	**2** (Protect **useful** and **important** records through management procedures)	**3** (Protect **useful** and **important** records through management procedures)
of **Loss** **or**	**Medium**	**4** (Recovery procedures for **important** records included in business continuity plan)	**5** (Reduce risk where possible; recovery procedures for **important** records included in business continuity plan)	**6** (Reduce risk; recovery procedures for **important** records included in business continuity plan)
Damage	**High**	**7** (Protect **vital** records; recovery procedures included in business continuity plan)	**8** (Reduce risk where possible; protect **vital** records; recovery procedures included in business continuity plan)	**9** (Reduce risk; protect **vital** records; recovery procedures included in business continuity plan)

Sample Impact/Probability Rating		
Facility	**Risks/Vulnerabilities**	**Impact/Probability Score**

Records and Information Risk Assessment
Site Survey

Date: _____   Surveyor: _____

Place:
Facility: _____   Room: _____
Location in Building: _____
Type of Building: _____
Roof Type & Condition: _____
Approx. Room Size: _____
Windows/Doors: _____
Loft or Mezzanine Storage: ☐ Yes   ☐ No
Locality Risk: _____

Climate:
High/Low Temperature Range: _____
Heating: ☐ Yes   ☐ No
Air-Conditioning: ☐ Yes   ☐ No
Humidity Control: ☐ Yes   ☐ No
Temperature/Humidity Monitoring: ☐ Yes   ☐ No

Lighting:
☐ Natural   ☐ Fluorescent   ☐ UV Control
☐ Incandescent   ☐ Direct Sunlight

Security:
Entry Alarms: ☐ Doors   ☐ Windows   ☐ Motion Sensors
Fire Alarms: ☐ Heat   ☐ Smoke
Automatic Extinguishers: _____
Type: _____   Location: _____
Portable Extinguishers: _____
Type: _____   Location: _____
Insurance: _____

Vulnerabilities:
Fire: _____
Electrical: _____   Heating: _____
Equipment: _____
Water: _____
Plumbing: _____
Moisture Accumulation: _____
Building Leaks: _____
Evidence of: ☐ Insects   ☐ Rodents   ☐ Humidity Extremes   ☐ Temperature Extremes   ☐ Mold/Mildew
Other: _____
       _____
       _____
       _____

Records and Information Risk Assessment
Site Survey (continued)

Records/Information Housing:

Record (1): _____   Media: _____

Personally Identifiable Information: ☐ Yes   ☐ No

Business Confidential: ☐ Yes   ☐ No

Original: ☐ Yes   ☐ No   Condition: _____

Container Enclosure Type: _____

Housing: _____   Type: _____

Specialty: ☐ Yes   ☐ No   Condition: _____

Existing Dispersal: ☐ Yes   ☐ No

Where: _____

Problems Noted: _____

Record (2): _____   Media: _____

Personally Identifiable Information: ☐ Yes   ☐ No

Business Confidential: ☐ Yes   ☐ No

Original: ☐ Yes   ☐ No   Condition: _____

Container Enclosure Type: _____

Housing: _____   Type: _____

Specialty: ☐ Yes   ☐ No   Condition: _____

Existing Dispersal: ☐ Yes   ☐ No

Where: _____

Problems Noted: _____

Electronic Equipment:

Type: _____   Info Media: _____

Use: _____

Brand/Model: _____

Vendor: _____   Serial #: _____

Standalone: ☐ Yes   ☐ No   Operating System: _____

Info Backup: ☐ Yes   ☐ No

Back-up Method: _____

Location: _____

Problems Noted: _____

Remarks:

_____

_____

_____

_____

_____

_____

_____

_____

_____

Vital Records Matrix

Record Identifier	Record	Location	Media	Electronic Application	Reference Activity	Personal or Confidential Information	Protection	Classification and Priority	Recovery Responsibility

Initial Damage Assessment Report

Facility Damaged: _____

Location: _____
_____
_____

(Attach map with clearly marked location and travel route to site, if needed.)

Describe Damage or Injuries: _____
_____
_____
_____

List Work Needed to Repair Damaged Site: _____
_____
_____
_____
_____

List Work That Has Been Completed: _____
_____
_____

(Attach activity report if any work has been completed.)

Estimated Cost: _____

(Develop a detailed breakdown of personnel, equipment, and materials for complete
damage assessment; include estimate of any loss of revenue.)

Notes/Comments: _____
_____
_____
_____
_____
_____
_____
_____

Damage Report Completed By: _____   **Date:** _____

Records and Information Damage Assessment Report

Facility: _____

Location: _____

Name of person in charge at site: _____   Phone/Pager: # _____

Directions to site: _____

Where and to whom to report: _____

Identification needed: ☐ Yes   ☐ No

Type of Damage: ☐ Fire   ☐ Smoke   ☐ Water   ☐ Chemical   ☐ Insect   ☐ Other

Localized: ☐ Yes   ☐ No   Entire facility: ☐ Yes   ☐ No

Extent of damage: ☐ Heavy   ☐ Moderate   ☐ Light

Description of damage: _____

_____

_____

_____

_____

Records and Information Damaged: _____

File housing damage: ☐ Yes   ☐ No   Describe: _____

Container damage: ☐ Yes   ☐ No   Describe: _____

Enclosure damage: ☐ Yes   ☐ No   Describe: _____

_____

         ☐ Vital   ☐ Confidential   ☐ Secure   Security Code: _____

Vital records classification: ☐ V1   ☐ V2   ☐ V3

Media: _____

Stabilization techniques necessary: _____

_____

_____

_____

Damage Category: ☐ Unharmed   ☐ Damaged—requires recovery   ☐ Destroyed/unsalvageable

Recovery Recommendations:

☐ Recovery service: _____   ☐ Internal

☐ Recovery service pack and transport: _____   ☐ Internal pack and transport

Number of internal personnel required: _____

Supplies needed: _____

Damage report completed by: _____   Date: _____

Index

About the Authors

Virginia A. Jones, CRM, FAI, is currently the records manager for Newport News Dept. of Public Utilities, Newport News, Virginia. Her background includes hands-on operations, management, consulting, writing, teaching, and training experience for over 40 years in the records and information management field. For over 20 years, she has also been principal of VAJones Associates, a records and information management consulting and training firm. Virginia is also an adjunct graduate course instructor in the School of Library and Information Science for Wayne State University.

Virginia is a member of several AIIM standards committees and a past member of the AIIM Standards Board. She is also a member of the U.S. delegation (TAG) to ISO TC 171, the international standards development committee for document management applications. She has been a project leader for several AIIM, ARMA, and ISO standards, including ANSI/ARMA 5-2010, *Vital Records Programs: Identifying, Managing, and Recovering Business-Critical Records,* and technical report development and revisions. Her work in national and international standards earned her the prestigious Thomas Bagg Excellence in Standards Award from AIIM International in 2007.

Virginia is the author of *Handbook of Microfilm Technology & Procedures* (QP Publishing) as well as a contributor to *The Information Manager's Toolkit* (ARMA International), *Records Management,* 8th ed. (Thompson Southwestern), and the *Encyclopedia of Library & Information Science* (Marcel Dekker, Inc.). She has contributed numerous articles on records and information management and micrographics concerns to national trade publications. Virginia currently serves on the Board of Regents of the Institute of Certified Records Managers. She is an active member of AIIM International (Old Dominion Chapter) and ARMA International (Tidewater Chapter) and has presented several papers at the national conferences for both associations. Virginia is a Fellow of ARMA International, a Fellow of AIIM International, and a current member of the Institute of Certified Records Managers.

Darlene Barber, CRM, is the Records Administrator for Newport News Shipbuilding, Newport News, Virginia. As a Certified Records Manager, she is responsible for the administration of the various components of the company's records management program and the operation of its vital records component. In addition to her records management responsibilities, Darlene is also a lead quality auditor, qualifying her to manage the planning and performance of quality system audits.

As an ARMA International Vital Records Task Force member, Darlene was a contributing writer of ANSI/ARMA 5-2003, *Vital Records Programs: Identifying, Managing, and Recovering Business-Critical Records.* She is an active member of the Tidewater Chapter of ARMA International and has served on the chapter board in various capacities. Darlene is also a speaker at local professional association meetings and in community college classrooms. She earned a Bachelor of Arts degree from the College of William and Mary in Williamsburg, Virginia.

About ARMA International

ARMA International is the leading professional organization for persons in the expanding field of records and information management.

As of May 2011, ARMA has about 10,000 members in the United States, Canada, and more than 30 other countries around the world. Within the United States, Canada, Japan, and Jamaica, ARMA has nearly 120 local chapters that provide networking and leadership opportunities through monthly meetings and special seminars.

The mission of ARMA International is to educate, advocate, and provide resources that enable professionals to manage information as a critical element of organizational operations and governance.

The ARMA International headquarters office is located in Overland Park, Kansas, in the Kansas City metropolitan area. Office hours are 8:30 A.M. to 5:00 P.M., Central Time, Monday through Friday.

ARMA International
11880 College Blvd, Suite 450
Overland Park, Kansas 66210
913.341.3808
Fax: 913.341.3742
headquarters@armaintl.org
www.arma.org